table of contents

KT-394-568

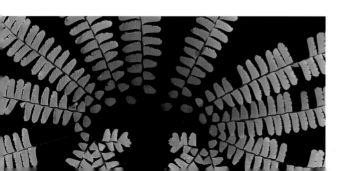

GEMSTONES

chapter 1

"Nature is not only all that
is visible to the eye…it also
includes the inner pictures of
the soul." — Edvard Munch

ORGANIC BEADED
jewelry

Susan Ray

©2005 Susan Ray
Published by

kp books
An Imprint of F+W Publications

700 East State Street • Iola, WI 54990-0001
715-445-2214 • 888-457-2873

Our toll-free number to place an order or obtain a free catalog is (800) 258-0929.

Arrow Springs®, Art Clay®, Syringe Silver™, Slow Dry Art Clay Silver™, Paste Type Silver™, Artistic Wire, Ltd.®, Badger® Balm, Beacon Glass Metal and More®, Beadalon®, Hot Stuff™, Cool Tool®, Creative Spirit Crafts®, Crystal Cottage Studio®, Darice® Charming Embellishments™, Dremel®, Faux Dichro® Liquid Glass™, Hi-Gloss™, Luminous Elements™, Pro's Choice Topcoat™, Fire Mountain Gems and Beads®, Dyna Mites™, Flecto® Varathane, Frantz Art Glass and Supply®, Future®, G-S Hypo-Tube Cement®, Halcraft USA Inc.®, Hilltribe®, Judikins, Inc®, Kai Scissors®, Karmul Studios®, Kemper® Klay Gun™, EZ-Squeeze Klay Gun™, Krylon®, Webbing Spray™, Luna Lights®, Memory Makers®, Nature Photo Bracelet™, EZ-Fit Photo Reduction Template™, Pearl Ex®, Pigmented Powders™, Super Copper™, Pinzart, Inc®, PMC® PMC3™, Crafter's Station and Torch®, Polyform Products Company®, PREMO!™, Granitex™, Powercord™, Pro's Choice Topcoat™, Rio Grande®, Rubber Stamps of Arkansas®, Sculpey Clay®, Super Slicer™, Glaze™, Super Flex™, Sculpey®, Texture Sheets™, Satin or Gloss Glaze™, Shutterfly®, Super Glue®, Susan Jones' Jones Tones® Micro-Cut Glitter®, Swarovski® Chaton™, Teflon®, The Beadery® ,The Clay Factory®, The Coiling Gizmo® Econo Winder™, Thompson®, Klyr-Fire™, Tupperware®, X-acto®

Library of Congress Catalog Number: 2005931486
ISBN: 0-87349-973-5
Edited by Candy Wiza
Designed by Emily Adler
Printed in China

Cover: Designer Sandi Webster, see page 33
Title page: Photo by Richard Pearce, see page 157

dedication

in memoriam:

- Regina Calvert, for her gentle sunshine.
- Jim Martin, whose eyes sparkled even when not behind the camera.
- Vivian Chevillon, MWS, for breaking every barrier with courage for us all.

and to:

- Doug Auburn, who spent his life in the noblest profession: teaching.

I would like to thank the following people for their individual contributions in bringing this book to life:

- Julie Stephani, once again, for her friendship and faith in me.
- Candy Wiza, my editor and project manager, for her intellectual sparring, creativity and laughter.
- KP Books and F+W Publications, for their continued support and gracious latitude.
- Richard Pearce, for his floral photographs that sing to the eye.
- Emily Adler, our graphic designer, for her visual enhancements to every page.
- Robert Best, for the studio photography that graces these pages.
- Juli Ikonomopoulos, for her unwavering commitment to make my ramblings understandable and brief. Juli, I can never thank you enough for setting what spilled from my heart into such discerning text. *Organic Beaded Jewelry* and *Easy Beaded Jewelry* could only become a reality because of your unwavering commitment to excellence.
- The amazing talents of polymer artists who filled these pages with magical projects: Marie Segal, syndee holt, Patricia Kimle, and Tracy Callahan.
- The creative musing of so many wonderfully talented jewelry designers: Sue Kwong, Karen Li, Jessica Italia, Eileen Feldman, Barbara Markoe, Sandi Webster, Cindy Vela, Nora Howe, Nancy Wolfe, Lynn Larkins, Tamara Knight, Ilene Baranowitz, Jeanne Holland and Wendy Mullane.
- The talented lampwork artists who once again gave so graciously of their work: Gary Haun, Tamara Knight, Roberta Ogborn, Karen Leonardo, Amy Caswell, Dave and Rebecca Jurgens.
- Memory Makers, for sharing their inspiration and photo bracelet with us.
- Halcraft, once again, for their encouragement, support and generosity.
- Coiling Gizmo, for providing their informative materials.
- Polyform Products Company, for their generosity with talent and product.
- Kevin, for his ever-patient understanding and love.
- Eric, for lighting my life with his every adventure.

"To live content with small means; to seek elegance rather than luxury, and refinement rather than fashion; to be worthy, not respectable, and wealthy, not, rich; to listen to stars and birds, babes and sages, with open heart; to study hard; to think quietly, act frankly, talk gently, await occasions, hurry never; in a word, to let the spiritual, unbidden and unconscious, grow up through the common - this is my symphony."
—*William Henry Channing*

acknowledgments

introduction

"To find the universal elements enough; to find the air and the water exhilarating; to be refreshed by a morning walk or an evening saunter; to be thrilled by the stars at night; to be elated over a bird's nest or a wildflower in spring - these are some of the rewards of the simple life."

— *John Burroughs*

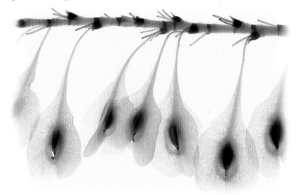

defining "Organic Jewelry"

or·gan·ic

Organic jewelry: 1) handmade, natural, intuitive 2) illuminating, imaginative, miraculous 3) innocent, artful, intimate 4) mimic 5) beauty, balance, harmony 6) energetic, intriguing, reflective 7) spiritual, protective, spherical 8) rejuvenating, reclamation, preservation 9) mystical, creative, resourceful 10) individual. Organic forms utilize or mimic nature in stones, leaves, insects, feathers, the stars and even the face of the moon, not just as an adjective, but also as an abstract, indicative of the very act of creation and discovery.

The jewelry presented in this book is from many diverse views of the definition of *organic* as seen by the eyes of the designer: some whimsical and laced with humor, others naturally tied to cultural backgrounds and ethnic diversities. It is not so much about what the jewelry is made of, but by the human spirit that guided the creation.

❀ **FYI** *All jewelry is measured without the clasp. All earrings are measured without the ear wire, the dangle only. If you use a different clasp or ear wire, your finished size will change. To increase length, add more beads. To decrease, remove a few beads. Always measure twice and crimp once!*

blue skies of taos necklace and bracelet ensemble

AFFLUENT

"Everybody needs beauty as well as bread, places to play in and pray in, where Nature may heal and give strength to body and soul alike." — *John Muir*

Designer: Eileen Feldman

Finished Size: Necklace: 18½"; Bracelet: 7½"

Expense: Over $50

Level of Expertise: Intermediate

Time to Complete: One week

necklace

supplies

Sterling silver and pearl clasp (preferably with large jump rings)

(4) 24" to 30" strands 18-gauge 7-strand flexible wire

8 to 10 sterling silver 3 mm x 2 mm crimp beads

Additional beads and findings itemized under each strand

tool box

Flat nose pliers

Round nose pliers

Wire cutters

Ruler

Crimping tool

tip *Store your beads in an egg carton or ice cube tray and label by letter. It will make your beading process easier and faster.*

	blue skies of taos - legend	strand 1	strand 2	strand 3	strand 4
A	Bali silver 3 mm spacers	17	8	11	18
B	White 5 mm pearls	14	10	2	6
C	Sterling silver 2 mm spacer beads	12	12	38	17
D	Beige 11/0 seed beads	10	12	9	67
E	Swarovski clear crystal 3 mm tapered beads	10	4	9	6
F	Swarovski dark sapphire 3 mm tapered beads	3	30	34	-
G	Swarovski dark sapphire 4 mm tapered beads	9	1	2	-
H	Swarovski light sapphire 6 mm round beads	6	24	-	-
I	Swarovski light topaz 6 mm tapered beads	6	-	7	11
J	Light champagne 9 mm flat pearls	5	-	5	9
K	Swarovski sapphire 12 mm tapered beads	2	-	-	-
L	Swarovski clear crystal 12 mm tapered beads	2	1	2	-
M	Bali silver 8 mm x 12 mm beads	2	-	-	-
N	Bali silver 13 mm bead	1	-	-	-
O	Swarovski sapphire 8 mm cubes	-	3	-	-
P	Bali silver 12 mm beads	-	1	-	-
Q	Bali silver 3 mm spacers	-	-	4	-
R	Bali silver 6 mm beads	-	-	2	10

necklace strand 1

Step-by-Step

See Multi-Strand Instructions, page 150.

1 Take one strand of flexible wire and insert and crimp wire in clasp.

2 Referring to the supplies list, add beads in the sequence that follows:

D-D-D-D-D-B-C-E-G-E-H-A-B-F-A-I-B-G-A-E-M-E-B-C-K-C-B-I-A-B-G-A-L-A-G-J-C-H-C-E-B-C-H-A-J-F-N-F-J-A-H-C-B-E-C-H-C-J-G-A-L-A-G-B-A-I-A-J-A-I-B-C-K-C-B-E-M-E-A-G-B-I-A-F-B-I-A-G-B-A-H-E-G-E-C-B-D-D-D-D-D

3 Insert the end into the other side of your clasp and crimp closed.

necklace strand 2

Step-by-Step

1 Take one strand of flexible wire and insert and crimp wire in clasp.

2 Referring to the supplies list, add beads in the sequence that follows:

D-D-D-D-D-D-D-G-F-F-B-E-C-F-C-E-B-A-H-H-H-H-H-B-A-F-F-F-C-O-C-F-F-F-C-L-C-F-F-F-C-O-C-F-F-F-A-B-H-H-H-H-H-H-P-H-H-H-B-A-F-F-F-F-F-C-O-C-F-F-F-F-F-F-A-B-H-H-H-H-H-B-A-B-H-H-H-H-H-B-A-F-F-F-A-B-E-C-F-C-E-F-D-D-D-D-D

3 Insert the end into the other side of your clasp and crimp closed.

necklace strand 3

Step-by-Step

1 Take one strand of flexible wire and insert and crimp wire in clasp.

2 Referring to the supplies list, add beads in the sequence that follows:

D-D-D-D-D-E-C-E-C-E-C-E-C-F-C-F-C-F-C-F-C-F-C-F-C-F-C-F-C-F-C-F-C-F-C-F-C-F-C-F-Q-J-Q-G-A-I-A-L-A-J-A-E-B-E-C-F-C-F-I-F-J-A-F-I-F-R-L-R-F-I-F-A-J-A-F-I-F-C-E-B-E-C-A-I-A-L-A-I-A-G-Q-J-Q-C-F-C-F-C-F-C-F-C-F-C-F-C-F-C-F-C-F-C-F-C-F-C-F-C-F-C-E-C-E-C-E-C-E-D-D-D

3 Insert the end into the other side of your clasp and crimp closed.

necklace strand 4

Step-by-Step

1 Take the last strand of flexible wire and insert and crimp wire in clasp.

2 Referring to the supplies list, add beads in the sequence that follows:

D-D-D-D-D-D-D-R-D-D-D-A-J-A-I-C-B-C-E-A-J-A-E-C-I-C-B-C-I-A-J-A-D-D-D-R-D-D-D-D-D-R-D-D-D-D-D-R-D-D-D-D-D-R-D-D-D-A-J-A-I-C-B-C-I-E-A-J-A-E-C-I-C-B-C-I-A-J-A-D-D-D-R-D-D-D-D-D-R-D-D-D-D-D-R-D-D-D-A-J-A-I-C-B-C-I-C-E-A-J-A-E-C-I-C-B-C-I-A-J-A-D-D-D-C-D-D-D-D-D-R-D-D-D-D-D-R-D-D-D-D-D-D-D

3 Insert the end into the other side of your clasp and crimp closed.

bracelet

supplies

1 sterling silver multi-strand toggle clasp

2 strands of .018-gauge 7-strand flexible wire cut into 12"-15" strands each

6 to 8 sterling silver 2 mm x 3 mm crimps

Additional beads and findings listed below under each strand

tool box

Flat nose pliers

Round nose pliers

Wire cutter

Crimping tool

Ruler

bracelet strand 1

supplies

10 Bali silver 3 mm spacers

10 sterling silver 2 mm spacers

10 beige 11/0 seed beads

8 Swarovski clear crystal 3 mm tapered beads

4 Swarovski dark sapphire 3 mm tapered beads

4 Swarovski dark sapphire 4 mm tapered beads

2 Swarovski light topaz 6 mm tapered beads

4 light champagne 9 mm flat pearls

2 Swarovski clear crystal 12 mm tapered beads

1 Swarovski sapphire 8 mm cube

Step-by-Step

See Multi-Strand Instructions, page 150.

1 Take one strand of flexible wire and insert and crimp wire in clasp.

2 Referring to the supplies list, add beads in the sequence that follows:

5 beige 11/0 seed beads
1 Swarovski dark sapphire 3 mm tapered bead
1 sterling silver 2 mm spacer
1 Swarovski clear crystal 3 mm tapered bead
1 Swarovski dark sapphire 3 mm tapered bead
1 sterling silver 2 mm spacer
1 Swarovski clear crystal 3 mm tapered bead
1 Swarovski dark sapphire 4 mm tapered bead
1 Bali silver 3 mm spacer
1 Swarovski clear crystal 3 mm tapered bead
1 Bali silver 3 mm spacer

1 light champagne 9 mm flat pearl
1 Bali silver 3 mm spacer
1 Swarovski clear crystal 12 mm tapered bead
1 Bali silver 3 mm spacer
1 light champagne 9 mm flat pearl
1 Bali silver 3 mm spacer
1 Swarovski dark sapphire 4 mm tapered bead
1 sterling silver 2 mm spacer
1 Swarovski light topaz 6 mm tapered bead
1 Swarovski clear crystal 3 mm tapered bead
1 Swarovski sapphire 8 mm cube

3 This is the center of your first strand. Now reverse your beading. Insert the end into the other side of your clasp and crimp closed.

bracelet strand 2

supplies

- 8 Bali silver 3 mm spacers
- 18 sterling silver 2 mm spacers
- 10 beige 11/0 seed beads
- 12 Swarovski clear crystal 3 mm tapered beads
- 4 Swarovski dark sapphire 3 mm tapered beads

- 4 Swarovski dark sapphire 4 mm tapered beads
- 2 Swarovski light topaz 6 mm tapered beads
- 2 Swarovski sapphire 12 mm tapered beads
- 2 light champagne 9 mm flat pearls
- 1 Swarovski sapphire 8 mm cube

Step-by-Step

1 Take one strand of flexible wire and insert and crimp wire in clasp.

2 Referring to the supplies list, add beads in the sequence that follows:

5 beige 11/0 seed beads
1 Swarovski clear crystal 3 mm tapered bead
1 sterling silver 2 mm spacer
1 Swarovski dark sapphire 3 mm tapered bead
1 sterling silver 2 mm spacer
1 Swarovski clear crystal 3 mm tapered bead
1 sterling silver 2 mm spacer
1 Swarovski dark sapphire 4 mm tapered bead
1 Bali silver 3 mm spacer
1 Swarovski clear crystal 3 mm tapered bead
1 Bali silver 3 mm spacer
1 Swarovski sapphire 12 mm tapered beads
1 Bali silver 3 mm spacer

1 Swarovski clear crystal 3 mm tapered bead
1 sterling silver 2 mm spacer
1 Swarovski dark sapphire 3 mm tapered bead
1 sterling silver 2 mm spacer
1 Swarovski clear crystal 3 mm tapered bead
1 sterling silver 2 mm spacer
1 Swarovski light topaz 6 mm tapered bead
1 sterling silver 2 mm spacer
1 light champagne 9 mm flat pearl
1 sterling silver 2 mm spacer
1 Swarovski dark sapphire 4 mm tapered bead
1 sterling silver 2 mm spacer
1 Swarovski clear crystal 3 mm tapered bead
1 Bali silver 3 mm spacer
1 Swarovski sapphire 8 mm cube

3 This is the center of your second strand. Now reverse your beading. Insert the end into the other side of your clasp and crimp closed.

queen's jester evening necklace and bracelet ensemble

"Art is born of the observation and investigation of nature."
— *Cicero (106 BC - 43 BC)*

Designer: Eileen Feldman

Overall Dimensions: Necklace: 16"

Overall Dimensions: Bracelet: 7½"

Expense: Over $50

Level of Expertise: Intermediate

Time to Complete: One week

supplies

2 clear 8 mm crystals

48" gold-filled 20-gauge dead-soft wire

12 gold-filled soldered 6 mm jump rings

1 gold-filled lobster clasp

Additional beads and findings listed below under each strand

tool box

Flat nose pliers

Round nose pliers

Wire cutters

Ruler

Adornment has been spoken as a universal language. It has captured our ethnic diversity, made tradition in our religions; it is recorded in our history and sung by our humanity.

necklace

supplies

10 Swarovski jet 10 mm crystals

10 gold-filled 4 mm Stardust beads

30 clear 3 mm crystals

10 gold-filled 3" head pins

10 gold-filled 6 mm x 8 mm corrugated Hogan beads

30 jet 3 mm cubes

40 Swarovski Chaton 1.5" crystal head pins

10 rose quartz 8 mm oval beads

28 jet 3 mm crystals

10 Swarovski clear 8 mm rounds

10 gold-filled 6 mm corrugated rondelles

5 rose quartz 20 mm x 14 mm beads

9 gold-filled 20-gauge dead-soft 6" wires

4 Swarovski white 12 mm simulated pearls

dangles

Make 10 each of the following groupings (but, do not close the tops). *See Dangles, page 154.*

group 1

1 Swarovski jet 10 mm crystal

1 gold-filled 4 mm Stardust bead

1 clear 3 mm crystal

1 gold-filled 3" head pin

group 2

1 gold-filled 6 mm x 8 mm corrugated Hogan bead

1 jet 3 mm cube

1 Swarovski Chaton 1.5" crystal head pin

group 3

1 clear 3 mm crystal

1 jet 8 mm cube

1 clear 3 mm crystal

1 Swarovski Chaton 1.5" crystal head pin

group 4

1 jet 3 mm crystal

1 rose quartz 8 mm oval bead

1 jet 3 mm crystal

1 Swarovski Chaton 1.5" crystal head pin

group 5

1 Swarovski clear 8 mm round

1 gold-filled 6 mm corrugated rondelle

1 Swarovski Chaton 1.5" crystal head pin

simulated pearl spacers

Make four **each** of the following (but, do not close the tops):

1 jet 3 mm crystal

1 Swarovski white 12 mm simulated pearl

1 jet 3 mm crystal

6" gold-filled 20-gauge dead-soft wire

rose quartz spacers

Make five **each** of the following groupings (but, do not close the tops):

1 jet 3 mm crystal

1 rose quartz 20 mm x 14 mm bead

1 jet 3 mm crystal

6" gold-filled 20-gauge dead-soft wire

Step-by-Step

See Basic Stringing Instructions, Single-Strand, page 146.

necklace blueprint

By following these steps, your necklace will be patterned below:
1 jump ring with 5 dangles
1 rose quartz 8 mm oval bead with two jet 3 mm crystals
1 jump ring with 5 dangles
1 Swarovski white 12 mm simulated pearl with two jet 3 mm crystals

1 Begin at One End

Start with your gold-filled lobster clasp. Cut a piece of wire approximately 6". Create a loop. String crystal bead through the wire, add jump ring and create a second loop. Cut away excess. This will attach the crystal to the jump ring on the end of the clasp.

2 Insert the Dangles

Take one dangle from each group (five total) and insert into jump ring, looping the head pins ends carefully. You've just made the first set of dangles.

3 Add the Rose Quartz Spacer

Take one prepared rose quartz spacer and insert into jump ring with sets of the dangles. Loop the wire around, closing the top. Take special care that your dangles are evenly spaced before closing.

4 Insert Dangles at the End of the Rose Quartz Spacer

At the opposite end, insert another jump ring. Insert a set of five dangles. Loop around jump ring and close.

5 Add the White Pearl Spacer

String the simulated white pearl spacer with another jump ring. Add another set of dangles inside this jump ring.

6 Make the Body of the Necklace

Repeat Steps 2, 3, 4 and 5 four times each.

7 End the Pattern

Repeat Steps 2, 3, and 4 one time each.

8 Close the Necklace

Cut a piece of wire approximately 6". String an 8 mm crystal bead through the wire. Close loop, adding the jump ring on the end of the clasp. (*See Wrapped Loop/Dangles, pages 152-156.*)

bracelet

supplies

2 clear 8 mm crystals

48" gold-filled 20-gauge dead-soft wire

12 gold-filled soldered 6 mm jump rings

1 gold-filled lobster clasp

5 Swarovski jet 10 mm crystals

5 gold-filled 4 mm Stardust beads

15 clear 3 mm crystals

5 gold-filled 3" head pins

5 gold-filled 6 mm x 8 mm corrugated Hogan beads

5 jet 3 mm cubes

20 Swarovski Chaton 1.5" crystal head pins

5 jet 8 mm cubes

20 jet 3 mm crystals

5 rose quartz 8 mm oval beads

5 Swarovski clear 8 mm rounds

5 gold-filled 6 mm corrugated rondelles

3 rose quartz 20 mm x 14 mm beads

2 white Swarovski 12 mm simulated pearls

tool box

Flat nose pliers

Round nose pliers

Wire cutter

Ruler

bracelet dangles

Make five **each** of the following groupings (but, do not close the tops):

group 1

1 Swarovski jet 10 mm crystal

1 gold-filled 4 mm Stardust bead

1 clear 3 mm crystal

1 gold-filled 3" head pin

group 2

1 gold-filled 6 mm x 8 mm corrugated Hogan bead

1 jet 3 mm cube

1 Swarovski Chaton 1.5" crystal head pin

group 3

1 clear 3 mm crystal

1 jet 8 mm cube

1 clear 3 mm crystal

1 Swarovski Chaton 1.5" crystal head pin

group 4

1 jet 3 mm crystal

1 rose quartz 8 mm oval bead

1 jet 3 mm crystal

1 Swarovski Chaton 1.5" crystal head pin

group 5

1 Swarovski clear 8 mm round

1 gold-filled 6 mm corrugated rondelle

1 Swarovski Chaton 1.5" crystal head pin

rose quartz spacers

Make three **each** of the following (but, do not close the tops):

1 jet 3 mm crystal

1 rose quartz 20 mm x 14 mm bead

1 jet 3 mm crystal

6" gold-filled 20-gauge dead-soft wire

simulated pearl spacers

Make two **each** of the following (but, do not close the tops):

1 jet 3 mm crystal

1 white Swarovski 12 mm simulated pearl

1 jet 3 mm crystal

6" gold-filled 20-gauge dead-soft wire

Step-by-Step

See Basic Stringing Instructions, Single-Strand, page 146. See Wrapped Loop Method, page 152.

bracelet blueprint

By following these steps, your bracelet will be patterned below:
1 jump ring with 5 dangles
1 rose quartz 8 mm oval bead with two jet 3 mm crystals
1 jump ring with 5 dangles
1 Swarovski 12 mm simulated white pearl with two jet 3 mm crystals

1 Start at One End

Cut a piece of wire approximately 6". Make a loop. Put an 8 mm crystal bead through the wire. Make another loop. Cut away excess wire. On the other end add a jump ring.

2 Insert the Dangles

Take one dangle from **each** group (five total) and insert into jump ring, looping the head pin ends carefully. You've just made the first set of dangles.

3 Add the Rose Quartz Spacer

Take one prepared rose quartz spacer and attach between the dangles. Take special care that your dangles are evenly spaced around the jump ring before closing.

4 Insert Dangles at the End of the Rose Quartz Spacer

At the opposite end, insert another jump ring. Insert a set of five dangles to the jump ring and close.

5 Add the White Pearl Spacer

In the dangles, place the simulated white pearl spacer with another jump ring at the opposite end. Add another set of dangles inside this jump ring.

6 Make the Body of the Bracelet

Repeat Steps 2, 3, 4, and 5 three times each.

7 End the Pattern

Repeat Steps 2, 3, and 4 one time each.

8 The Bracelet

Measure the bracelet against your wrist before you end and adjust accordingly. Cut a piece of wire approximately 6". Make a loop. String an 8 mm crystal bead through the wire. Make a second loop. Add jump ring. The final jump ring will be used at the other end of the lobster claw closure.

faux tourmaline bracelet

SIMPLE

"The beauty of Mother Nature is her ability to make complex things appear simple." — Louis E. Samuels, M.D.

Designer: Nora Howe

Lampwork Artist: Karen Leonardo

Finished Size: 7", without clasp

Expense: $50 - $100

Level of Expertise: Beginner to Intermediate

Time to Complete: One weekend

supplies

2 green 8 mm potato pearls

2 white 8 mm potato pearls

18 sterling silver 3 mm rondelle spacers

10 sterling silver 3 mm rondelle spacers

8 unakite 3 mm round spacers

2 amber sunrise faux tourmaline 12 mm lampwork bumpies

2 mystical ruby faux tourmaline 10 mm x 5 mm oval lampwork bumpies

1 sterling silver twisted toggle set

Roll of 20-gauge sterling silver wire

10 hand-cut briolettes in faceted teardrop and semi-teardrop shapes from 8 mm x 6 mm to 16 mm x 12 mm in the following colors: garnet, amethyst, labradorite, smoky quartz, hessonite, carnelian, iolite, rose quartz, rainbow moonstone, golden rainbow fluorite.

tool box

Flat nose pliers

Round nose pliers

Wire cutters

Ruler

Due to hand cutting, each of the gemstones has an individual size and shape. Measure your wrist and work your design accordingly.

Step-by-Step

1 Cut 6" piece of sterling silver wire. Create loop. Attach first loop to the end of toggle. String one spacer, one gemstone, and another spacer. Create second loop. *(See Wrapped Loop Method, page 152.)*

2 Continue adding gemstones and lampwork beads until your bracelet achieves proper length. Create last loop and attach to the other end of toggle.

Feminine in structure, organic forms can represent the notion of reclamation, shelter and protection.

island princess necklace

FORM

"I perhaps owe having become a painter to flowers." — Claude Monet

Designer: Sue Kwong and Karen Li

Finished Size: 16", without clasp

Expense: Less than $50

Level of Expertise: Beginner to Intermediate

Time to Complete: One day

supplies

1 orchid pendant, approximately 2" wide *with 4-sided looped bail

1 strand light green turquoise 17 mm x 13 mm ovals

7 Swarovski pink 4 mm bicones

18 white 4 mm freshwater pearls

3 white 8 mm freshwater pearls

7 white 6 mm freshwater pearls

2 white 2 mm freshwater pearls

32" of 19-strand .018 mm gauge flexible wire

4" sterling silver chain

2 sterling silver 4 mm spacers

19 sterling silver 24-gauge 1½" head pins

3 sterling silver 3" pieces of half-hard 24-gauge wire

4 sterling silver 3 mm x 2 mm crimp beads

1 sterling silver toggle set

*Fire Mountain Gems

tool box

Chain nose pliers

Round nose pliers

Criming pliers

Wire cutters

The beauty of the orchids is captured forever by poly resin preservation methods and from the genuine orchid. I softened the palette by adding white pearls. — Sue Kwong

To make this a beginner's project, omit the pearl and crystal cascade that suspends from the orchid. If you want to make the cascade, make sure that your orchid comes with a bail that has four loops. Make the cascade and attach to the orchid pendant's bail loop first (Step 4) to make assembly easier.

Step-by-Step

attach the toggle clasp

1 Cut two 16" pieces of flexible wire. String a 4 mm sterling silver spacer bead, crimp bead and one toggle end. Bring wire back through the crimp and spacer bead. Crimp your bead. Repeat with the other wire. You now have two wires with the toggle clasps attached.

make the necklace

1 String a light green turquoise oval bead and a 4 mm white freshwater pearl. Repeat pattern seven times ending with two white 4 mm freshwater pearls. Repeat for the other piece of wire.

2 String a crimp bead and take wire through the loop in the orchid's bail and back through the crimp bead. Crimp. Repeat for the other wire. You now have the necklace without the cascade completed.

make the cascade

1 Cut the 4" sterling silver chain into two pieces, one 1½" long and one 2½" long. Using head pins, attach three 6 mm white freshwater pearls, one 8 mm white freshwater pearl, and three pink 4 mm Swarovski bicones to the shorter sterling silver chain with the wrapped loop method. *(See Basic Stringing Instructions, Wrapped Looped Method, page 152.)*

2 String a light green turquoise oval and one 2 mm white freshwater pearl onto a head pin. Attach to the bottom of the chain with the wrapped loop method. With the head pins, attach the remaining pearls, crystals, and turquoise in the same manner onto the longer sterling silver chain. Attach the two sterling silver chains (cascade) onto the bail loop with the wrapped loop method.

a little piece of paradise necklace

FUNCTION

"What makes a river so restful to people is that it doesn't have any doubt - it is sure to get where it is going, and it doesn't want to go anywhere else."
— *Hal Boyle*

Designer: Jessica Italia

Finished Size: Top strand, 14"; bottom strands, 15", without clasp

Expense: $50 - $100

Level of Expertise: Beginner

Time to Complete: One day

supplies

47 beige 8 mm x 10 mm freshwater button pearls

115 mauve 3 mm x 4 mm freshwater button pearls

115 gold 3 mm x 4 mm freshwater button pearls

1 sterling silver 12 mm x 32 mm hook and clasp set

6 sterling silver 2 mm x 2 mm crimp beads

60" of 7-strand .018 mm gauge flexible wire

tool box

Wire cutters

Chain nose pliers

Ruler

Crimping tool

Step-by-Step

See Basic Stringing Instructions, Multi-Strand Necklace and Bracelet, pages 146-151.

1 Cut one 18" piece of flexible wire. Cut two 19" pieces of flexible wire.

2 Individually, string a crimp bead on all three strands of wire and crimp to one end of hook clasp set.

3 String (47) 8 mm x 10 mm pearls on 18" strand of wire and crimp to opposite end of clasp set.

4 String (115) 3 mm x 4 mm pearls to one 19" strand of wire and crimp.

5 Repeat Step 4 and twist strand around other 19" strand before crimping to clasp.

The "organic" whole denotes a unified structure. A simple body of great complexity.

ariel's gift

BEAUTY

"Climb the mountains and get their good tidings. Nature's peace will flow into you as sunshine flows into trees. The Winds will blow their own freshness into you, and the storms their energy while cares will drop away from you like the leaves of Autumn." — *John Muir (1838-1914)*

Designer: Sue Kwong and Karen Li

Finished Size: 15", without clasp

Expense: Less than $50

Level of Expertise: Beginner - Intermediate

Time to Complete: One day

supplies

1 strand red coral (approx.) 24 mm x 11 mm briolettes

1 abalone (approx.) 2½" x 1¼" pendant

8 peacock 4 mm freshwater pearls

4 Hilltribe silver 3 mm beads (stop beads)

2 sterling silver 4 mm spacers (stop beads)

2 sterling silver 2 mm x 2 mm crimp beads

22" piece of 7-strand .018" flexible wire

3" of 7-strand Tiger Tail .010" flexible wire

1 sterling silver toggle set (extra "O" ring is optional)

1 spool 24-gauge sterling silver wire

tool box

Chain nose pliers

Round nose pliers

Wire cutter

Crimping pliers (optional)

Hemostat

Ruler

Jeweler's glue (or Super glue)

One strand of coral briolettes usually comes in 15" to 16" length. Consider purchasing more than one strand if you would like a longer finished length of 16" to 17". This also would give you plenty of replacements for any damaged briolettes.

tip

Step-by-Step

plan your necklace

1 Lay out the coral briolettes. Place the larger and prettier pieces toward the center of your necklace. Planning your necklace will you give you better results.

Note: You will have a chance to pick through and throw away any unsightly or damaged beads.

2 Tie a knot at the end of your 22" flexible wire. String the coral briolettes (starting with the briolettes at the end) until you reach the center of the necklace.

make the loop for the pendant

1 Use eight 4 mm peacock colored pearls for the loop.

2 Using the 3" Tiger Tail wire, string the pearls on the wire. String one end of the wire through the hole in the pendant, bringing both ends of the wire to the back of the pendant, and loosely tie a knot.

3 String the pendant onto your wire with the coral briolettes. Now is the time to adjust the size of the loop. If the loop is too long, take off a pearl or two. If it is too short, add a pearl or two.

4 Add a few coral briolettes next to the pendant to get an idea of what the necklace will look like. Once you are satisfied with the results, tie a square or surgical knot in the back of the pendant just below the hole. Dab a little Super glue or jeweler's glue on the knot to keep it secure. Once the glue is dry, snip the ends of the wire.

5 Finish stringing the coral briolettes. Adjust the necklace to make sure that both ends are even. Try it around your neck, allowing for the clasp, and make sure that it is the desired length.

finish the necklace

1 Make "connectors" for the toggle clasps. This step is optional. You can omit making the connectors and finish the necklace by using the basic instructions for adding a clasp *(see Findings and Closures, page 153)*. For each connector (two are used in this necklace) use a 3" piece of 24-gauge sterling silver wire and make one wrapped loop. *(See Wrapped Loop Method, page 152.)*

2 String one 4 mm sterling silver spacer bead and one end of the toggle clasp. Make another wrapped loop. On your necklace, string two 3 mm Hilltribe silver beads, one 4 mm sterling silver bead, crimp bead and the loop in your connector. Take the wire back through all beads and crimp. You have completed one end of the clasp.

3 Repeat on the other end. To give the necklace more versatility, add another "O" ring to the clasp. The "O" ring is connected by the wrapped loop method.

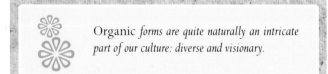
Organic *forms are quite naturally an intricate part of our culture: diverse and visionary.*

paradise necklace

SERENITY

" I decided that if I could paint that flower in a huge scale, you could not ignore its beauty." — Georgia O'Keeffe

Designer: Sandi Webster

Lampwork Artist: Karen Leonardo

Finished Size: 18"

Expense: $50 - $100

Level of Expertise: Beginner - Intermediate

Time to Complete: One day

supplies

1 light turquoise 35 mm diameter lampwork rose pendant

25 rainbow obsidian 6 mm round beads (5 for the pendant cascade)

20 rainbow obsidian 12 mm x 14 mm faceted briolettes (2 for the pendant cascade)

12 rainbow obsidian 10 mm x 12 mm faceted briolettes

22" of 49-strand .024 mm gauge flexible wire

2 sterling silver 3 mm crimp beads

1 sterling silver 13.5 mm lobster-claw clasp

1 sterling silver 3" section of 6.3 mm cable chain, plus 1 or 2 links

5 sterling silver 1½" fancy ball-tip headpins

2 sterling silver 10" pieces of 24-gauge wire

tool box

Round nose pliers

Crimping tool

Side cutter

Ruler

Step-by-Step

1 Center the flower pendant onto the flexible wire.

2 On one side of the necklace, add one 6 mm round rainbow obsidian bead, three 12 mm x 14 mm rainbow obsidian briolettes, one 6 mm rainbow obsidian round bead and three 10 mm x 12 mm rainbow obsidan briolettes. Repeat this pattern until you have used nine large and six small briolettes. Finish with five of the 6 mm round beads. Repeat on other side of necklace.

3a String crimp bead on end of necklace. Add one or two links of cable chain. Run flexible wire back through the crimp bead and several 6 mm rainbow obsidian beads. Crimp and add lobster-claw clasp with heavy sterling jump ring onto the cable link.

3b Repeat on other side, adding the 3" length of chain after the crimp bead. This side of the necklace will have the extension chain on it. Finish end of chain with wire-wrapped briolette or stack of the 6 mm round beads sitting atop head pin. See Step 5 for how to wrap a briolette.

4a Make the cascade: Use 24-gauge sterling silver wire and 6.3 mm sterling cable chain. Slide wire through holes in back of flower pendant and wrap down and around the flat "taplet" back.

4b Twist the ends of wire together snugly against the flat taplet portion of the bead. Add two pieces of the chain (one about ¾" in length and the other about 1¼") sliding the chain over the wire ends. Twist wire again and trim excess.

5a Add the briolettes to the cascade. To wrap briolette, take 7" of 24-gauge sterling silver wire and insert through bead.

5b Make a simple wrap with the short end of the wire and trim close to wrap.

5c Using chain nose pliers, make the first half of a loop, attach to the end of the chain and finish wrapping. Keep wrapping snug against the briolette. Trim excess wire, if needed. Repeat with second briolette on the other chain.

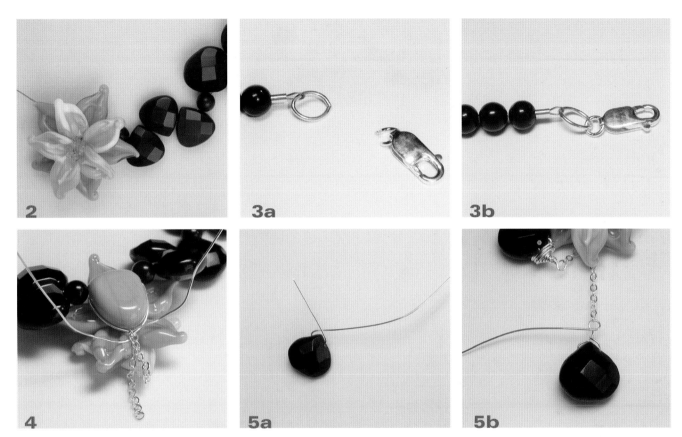

2

3a

3b

4

5a

5b

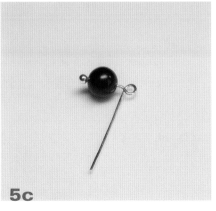

5c

6 Add the small round beads to the cascade. Make five "drops" using 6 mm rainbow obsidian beads and sterling silver ball-tip head pins. Slide bead onto head pin and make first half of a simple wrapped loop. Slip through chains at various spots and check how your placement looks. When you are satisfied with the placement, complete the wrap.

BEADS

chapter 2

bead influence

Amethyst = Love
Aventurine = Good Luck
Blue Gold = Calm
Crystal = Purity
Garnet = Romance
Jasper = Harmony
Multi = Unity
Rose Quartz = Balance
Sodalite = Tranquility
Tiger Eye = Peace
Turquoise = Healing
Unakite = Trust

"It is not the language of painters but the language of nature which one should listen to... The feeling for the things themselves, for reality, is more important than the feeling for pictures."
— *Vincent van Gogh*

desert sands necklace and bracelet

DRAMATIC

"Look deep into nature, and then you will understand everything better."
— *Albert Einstein*

Designer: Sandi Webster

Finished Size: 15", without clasp and extension chain

Expense: $50 - $100

Level of Expertise: Beginner

Time to Complete: One day

necklace

supplies

1 blue-green dolomite 24 mm x 32 mm carved scarab bead

3 blue-green Egyptian faience 14 mm x 12 mm carved scarab beads

2 citrine (approx.) 16 mm x 25 mm free-form nuggets

2 citrine 12 mm x 18 mm rough side-drilled nuggets

1 gold coral 14 mm x 22 mm tube bead

3 Peruvian turquoise 12 mm rondelles

1 Peruvian turquoise 18 mm puffed round disc bead

1 vintage copper 14 mm round bead

1 tiger's-eye 14 mm round bead

2 African copper 10 mm x 6 mm spiral beads

4 pyrite 12 mm round beads

3 black onyx 6 mm round beads

2 blue-green turquoise 6 to 7 mm round beads

5 topaz 8/0 glass seed beads

2 citrine 8 mm rondelles

2 brown jasper 3 mm beads

4 gold coral 7 mm round beads

1 gold coral 4 mm x 14 mm tube bead

2 sterling silver 22 mm conical "pendants"

2 sterling silver 14 mm spiral drops

2 sterling silver 22 mm tall "pyramid" pendants

1 copper 3 mm round bead

2 sterling silver 10 mm square bead caps

1 sterling silver round 2 mm bead

1 sterling silver 13.5 mm lobster-claw clasp

20" of 49-strand 26 lb. flexible wire

2 sterling silver 3 mm crimp beads

1 sterling silver 2" headpin

4" sterling silver 18-gauge wire

tool box

Round nose pliers

Side cutters

Crimping pliers

Flat nose pliers

File

Hammer

Ruler

---

tip

"Since you may not be able to find the exact same beads and pendants used in this design, be adventurous and use things that appeal to you. Use your imagination and have fun creating!" — Sandi Webster

Step-by-Step

See Basic Instructions, Single-Strand, page 146.

2 Begin adding beads on both sides of pendant. Each side of the necklace can be slightly different, so mix the beads into pleasing patterns, keeping a watchful eye on spacing and balance. Specifically used here, **Side 1**: 7 mm gold coral bead, Peruvian turquoise rondelle, sterling pyramid pendant, small faience scarab bead, tiny topaz seed bead, citrine nugget, round turquoise bead, sterling spiral pendant, black onyx bead, gold coral tube, brown jasper, rough citrine drop, brown jasper bead, sterling conical bead, large copper bead, onyx bead, spiraled copper bead, scarab bead, and pyrite bead. **Side 2**: round gold coral bead, Peruvian turquoise bead, sterling pyramid pendant, pyrite bead, scarab bead, 7 mm round gold coral, sterling round spiral, round turquoise, citrine rondelle, 14 mm tiger's-eye bead, topaz seed bead, rough citrine drop, topaz seed bead, Peruvian opal puffed disk, citrine rondelle, copper spiral bead, pyrite bead, round gold coral bead, citrine nugget, black onyx, pyrite and topaz seed bead.

3 When you are satisfied with bead placement, add sterling crimp bead on one end of wire. Run wire through link of sterling cable chain and back through crimp bead. Add lobster-claw clasp to link of chain with heavy-weight jump ring. Repeat on other side, but add 2" to 3" of sterling cable chain for extender instead of the clasp.

4 Add a decorative bead to end of sterling chain. (I used a gold coral tube bead which has been topped by a sterling accent bead.) Add beads to sterling head pin and make half of a basic wrapped loop. Add to end of chain and complete the loop.

make the pendant

1 Using round nose pliers and 4" of 18-gauge sterling wire, make a 10 mm coil at one end of the wire. Add one square sterling bead. Slide down the large scarab bead so it sits atop the square bead and coiled spiral. Add square bead and tiny copper bead to top of pendant. Finish by making a basic wrapped loop. *(See Basic Wraped Loop Instructions, page 152.)* Slide pendant onto the flexible wire and center.

bracelet

supplies

1 carved 30 mm x 18 mm dolomite scarab bead

2 free-form citrine 12 mm x 18 mm nuggets

2 "rough" citrine (approx.) 10 mm x 20 mm nugget drops

3 gold coral 12 mm to 13 mm x 4 mm cylinders

3 gold coral 7 mm rounds

2 Swarovski silver-gray 10 mm pearls

4 citrine 5 mm faceted rondelles

2 sterling 6 mm to 7 mm flat saucer beads

1 golden tiger's-eye 14 mm round bead

4 turquoise 6 mm to 7 mm rounds

1 turquoise 7 mm heishi bead

2 sterling silver 23 mm (approx.) pyramid pendants

2 hand-coiled sterling silver 14 mm diameter (approx.) spirals

8 sterling silver 1½" head pins

3 sterling silver 3 mm rounds

1 10" piece of 26 lb. flexible cord

1 sterling silver 15 mm toggle clasp set

2 sterling silver 3 mm crimp beads

12" sterling silver 18-gauge wire

tool box

Round nose pliers

Side cutters

Crimping pliers

Flat nose pliers

Ruler

Hammer

File

Finished Size: 6½", without toggle clasp

Expense: $50 - 100

Level of Expertise: Beginner - Intermediate

Time to Complete: One day

✿ tip *You may be able to find spiral pendants that you can simply purchase. (See Fire Mountain Gems, Resources.)*

Step-by-Step

1 String scarab focal bead on the flexible wire. Make the spiral pendants, following instructions 2a through 2c.

2a Cut an 8" piece of 18-gauge sterling silver wire and file ends. Using round nose pliers, make a tiny loop at one end.

2b Use a flat nose pliers to hold the coil in your right hand. Using your left thumb to guide the wire, press the wire up parallel with the edge of the pliers. Begin coiling the wire into a fairly tight spiral. Continue in this manner. You will have to reposition the pliers as your coil gets larger. Coils should be about ½" in diameter.

2c When the coil is about ½" in diameter, bend the wire and make a basic wrapped loop. Make two of these for the bracelet. *(See Basic Wrapped Loop Instructions, page 152.)* Hammer the coils lightly to harden the wire.

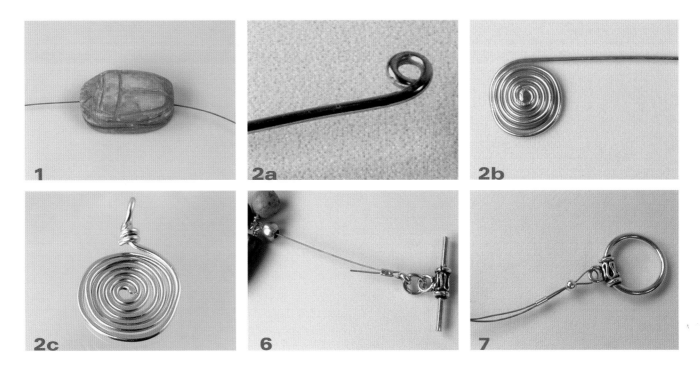

3 Begin adding other beads next to the scarab. Hand coil the gold coral round beads, tubes and a couple of the round turquoise beads on sterling head pins so they can be hung on the flexible wire like tiny pendants. The gold coral cylinders sit atop 3 mm sterling silver rounds.

4 On one side of scarab, string the following: one sterling silver flat saucer bead, one turquoise bead (coiled on head pin) pyramid bead, citrine nugget, round turquoise bead, one gold coral round bead (hand coiled on head pin) citrine rondelle, citrine rough drop, citrine rondelle, sterling coiled "pendant," Swarovski pearl, gold coral cylinder, turquoise round (hand coiled on head pin) and small sterling bead.

5 String other half of bracelet as follows: one sterling flat saucer, gold coral cylinder (hand coiled on sterling head pin) Swarovski pearl, sterling silver coiled "pendant," two gold coral beads (hand coiled on head pins) citrine rondelle, citrine rough drop, citrine rondelle, turquoise round, citrine nugget, sterling silver pyramid pendant, tiger's-eye bead, gold coral cylinder (hand coiled on sterling head pin) and turquoise heishi.

6 Add a crimp bead along with the bar of the toggle clasp. Add a few small, heavy-gauge jump rings if your toggle does not have some chain links already attached to it. Or, add a few tiny sterling silver beads next to the last bead on the bracelet before you attach the toggle with the crimp bead. The toggle bar must have lead on it to facilitate closing.

7 Repeat at other end with ring portion of toggle clasp. Slip the crimp on the flexible wire and add one 2 mm sterling silver round before slipping the wire through the ring on the toggle. Run flexible wire back through the silver bead, the crimp, and a few of the beads on bracelet. Adjust and close the crimp bead with pliers. Cut away excess wire.

playin' in ma's button jar bracelet

INNOCENT

"You must not know too much or be too precise or scientific about birds and trees and flowers and watercraft; a certain free-margin, and even vagueness - ignorance, credulity - helps your enjoyment of these things."
— Henry David Thoreau

Designer: Jessica Italia

Finished Size: 7½", without clasp

Expense: Less than $50

Level of Expertise: Beginner

Time to Complete: One day

Color Palette: Marriage of Metals - gold, silver, copper

supplies

3 vintage ivory 8 mm x 8 mm round shank buttons

5 vintage glass-etched jet 10 mm x 10 mm faceted shank buttons

2 vintage crystal 10 mm x 10 mm square shank buttons

1 vintage glass-etched brown 24 mm x 26 mm triangle shank button

9½" antique gold 5 mm ring chain link

tool box

Round nose pliers

Chain nose pliers

Wire cutters

Ruler

 tip   *Use both pliers when opening links in chain to attach button shanks.*

Step-by-Step

1 Create a 1½" loop with one end of chain, attach by opening a link and adding it to another (1½" apart).

2 Attach large triangle button to opposite end of chain link to create the closure for bracelet.

3 By opening rings on chain link, attach buttons about ½" apart. Re-close ring after every button attached.

4 Starting at loop end, attach jet, ivory, jet, crystal, jet, ivory, jet, crystal, jet, ivory.

autumn moon pendant necklace

AGED

"There is a pleasure in the pathless woods, There is a rapture on the lonely shore, There is society, where none intrudes, By the deep sea, and music in its roar: I love not man the less, but Nature more." — Lord Byron

Designer: Susan Ray

Lampwork Artist: Tamara Knight

Finished Size: 16½" (shortest strand) to 24", without clasp

Expense: More than $100

Level of Expertise: Beginner

Time To Complete: One weekend

supplies

22 copper matte 6/0 seed beads

225 copper russet matte 11/0 seed beads

30 sunstone 4 mm rounds*

32 black glass 6 mm to 8 mm cubes/vary

2 petrified wood agate 15 mm x 7 mm tubes

16 silver 6 mm x 7 mm ribbed bicones

8 red jasper 5 mm x 8 mm faceted rondelles*

8 Indian agate 5 mm x 8 mm faceted rondelles*

6 sunstone 11 mm x 7 mm faceted rectangles*

4 Chinese carnelian 13 mm rounds*

2 amber sheep horn 12 mm x 7 mm tubes*

1 Norwegian Bokmal hematite 14 mm x 12 mm nugget*

6 Siam furnace 9 mm rounds

6 mahogany obsidian 15 mm x 7 mm twisted tubes*

8 blue/purple 6 mm x 5 mm potato pearls

5 crazy lace agate 17 mm x 12 mm faceted rectangles*

2 red transparent 6 mm x 8 mm abacus rondelles

2 orange furnace 9 mm rounds

4 brown 5 mm x 9 mm pebble shells

2 mahogany obsidian 10 mm x 10 mm diamonds*

2 poppy jasper 15 mm x 7 mm twisted tubes*

2 amber sheep horn 4 mm x 8 mm rondelles

1 carved bone 45 mm pendant

1 purple amethyst 9 mm lampwork round

1 sterling silver 3 mm faceted round

1 silver Czech fire 4 mm faceted round

1 silver 4 mm x 8 mm double spacer

1 sterling silver 3" headpin

1 silver wire coiled

1½" sterling silver chain link

6 sterling 2 mm x 3 mm crimp beads

1 sterling silver lobster claw clasp

1 sterling silver jump ring

64" of 7-strand .018 mm gauge flexible wire

4" bollo chain

*Available through Crystal Cottage Studio, see Resource Directory on page 160.

tool box

Wire cutters

Flat nose pliers

Round nose pliers

tip

When making a pendant from an object without a hole, use silver wire to secure it. Make a loop twice as large as you will require. Wrap the wire several times around the object, continuing to make loop twice the size. Once you have done this three or four times, leave about one extra inch of wire and cut the rest away. Holding the loop, twist the wire around and around creating a wire figure eight. When the wire is taut, wrap short end at midpoint around the twist. Voila! A pendant!

Step-by-Step

See Basic Stringing Instructions, Multi-Strand Necklace and Bracelet, page 150.

When wrapping sterling wire to form a secure tie for stringing an object, start by creating a loop twice as long than the bead requires. Place the loop around the object and turn it into a simple figure eight. Twist, creating a hanger for the bead. Make sure the wire is tightly wrapped about the bead. The upper portion of the figure eight acts as the hanging wire.

passion choker

GRACE

"Nature is also man's teacher. She unfolds her treasures to his search, unseals his eyes, illumes his mind, and purifies his heart; an influence breathes from all the sights and sounds of her existence" — Alfred Billings Street

Designer: Jessica Italia

Finished Size: 13¾", without clasp

Expense: $50 - $100

Level of Expertise: Beginner

Time to Complete: One day

supplies

46 brown 3 mm x 6 mm genuine leather heishe beads

24 Norwegian Bokmal sterling silver 7 mm Bali star spacers

18 red 10 mm x 14 mm African vaseline trade abacus rondelles

3 red 5 mm x 14 mm African vaseline trade abacus rondelles

2 sterling silver 2 mm x 2 mm crimp beads

1 sterling silver 11 mm x 20 mm hook-and-clasp set

18" of 19-strand .015 diameter flexible wire

tool box

Wire cutters

Chain nose pliers

Adhesive tape

Crimping tool

Step-by-Step

See Basic Stringing Instructions, Single-Strand Necklace, page 150.

1 Tape one end of 18" flexible beading wire.

2 String one 5 mm x 14 mm red trade bead, one leather heishe and one 5 mm x 14 mm trade bead.

3 String as follows: heishe, spacer, heishe, spacer, heishe, spacer and heishe.

4 String a 10 mm x 14 mm trade bead, heishe, trade bead, heishe and trade bead.

5 Repeat Steps 3 and 4 twice and repeat Step 3 to finish.

6 String a crimp bead to finished side and crimp to one end of hook clasp.

7 Remove tape from opposite end, string a heishe and a 5 mm x 14 mm trade bead.

8 Repeat Steps 3 through 6 to finish.

tip *Take apart old, outdated jewelry and reuse beads to create new, unique designs.*

santa fe bracelet

PRIMITIVE

Designer: Jessica Italia

Finished Size: 5¾", without clasp

Expense: Less than $50

Level of Expertise: Beginner

Time to Complete: One day

supplies

34 red coral 5 mm x 8 mm antique premium short coral branches

6 green turquoise 2 mm x 4 mm Chinese chips

6 silver 6 mm x 11 mm leaves

1 antique turquoise 18 mm x 24 mm nugget

1 sterling silver with coral 9 mm x 11 mm triangle charm

1 sterling silver with coral 8 mm x 20 mm S-hook clasp set

10" of 7-strand .018 mm gauge flexible wire

2 sterling silver 2 mm x 2 mm crimp beads

tool box

Wire cutters

Chain nose pliers

Adhesive tape

Crimping tool

> tip
>
> *The vintage turquoise nugget and red coral used in this piece were taken from a necklace belonging to my great aunt. I made my mother, my sisters and myself a special piece of jewelry by recycling the beads into bracelets we all can enjoy.*

Step-by-Step

See Basic Stringing Instructions, Single-Strand Bracelet, page 146.

1 Tape one end of 10" flexible wire.

2 String on antique turquoise nugget for focal bead.

3 String two coral, one chip, one coral, one leaf, two coral.

4 Repeat Step 3 twice and add two coral to finish.

5 String a crimp bead and crimp to one end of S-hook clasp set.

6 Remove tape and repeat Steps 1 through 5.

7 Open the end of S-hook clasp (which will remain closed) and add charm.

howlin' at the moon choker

CASUAL

"I thank you God for this most amazing day, for the leaping greenly spirits of trees, and for the blue dream of sky and for everything which is natural, which is infinite, which is yes." — e.e. cummings

Designer: Jessica Italia

Finished Size: 12½", without clasp

Expense: Less than $50

Level of Expertise: Intermediate

Time to Complete: One day

supplies

104 tea rose matte hex-cut beads

16 silver 4 mm x 5 mm bicone spacers

10 smoke 3 mm x 8 mm glass rings

3 burnt orange carnelian 4 mm x 6 mm faceted rondelles

8 hematite 7 mm x 7 mm stars

3 glass-speckled 6 mm x 6 mm cubes

2 gold 6 mm x 6 mm potato freshwater pearls

1 pewter 11 mm x 14 mm moon charm

2 brass 25 mm round washers

1 antique gold 6 mm split ring

3 sterling silver 2 mm x 2 mm crimp beads

1 sterling silver 16 mm toggle set

36" of 7-strand .018 mm gauge flexible wire

tool box

Chain nose pliers

Wire cutters

Crimping tool

Ruler

Step-by-Step

1 Cut two pieces of 10" flexible wire and one piece of 9" flexible wire.

2 String 16 tea rose hex-cut beads to 10" wire and loop through a washer. String a spacer and a crimp bead, pull tight towards spacer and crimp.

3 Add a glass ring (to cover crimp bead) string spacer, six hex-cut, star, two hex-cut, pearl, four hex-cut, spacer, six hex-cut, ring, star, two hex-cut, cube, four hex-cut, spacer, six hex-cut, ring, star, two hex-cut, rondelle, four hex-cut, spacer, crimp bead, ring and a spacer.

4 String wire through one end of toggle set and back through spacer, crimp, ring and spacer. Using the tip of chain nose pliers, adjust ring to crimp the crimp bead tightly to wire.

5 Repeat Steps 2 through 4.

6 Repeat Step 2 using 9" flexible wire (string downward from previous steps).

7 Add a ring (to cover crimp bead) string spacer, six hex-cut, star, two hex-cut, rondelle, four hex-cut, spacer, crimp bead, glass ring, spacer, four hex-cut, cube, two hex-cut, split ring, star and six hex-cut.

8 Loop through other washer and with the excess wire, string it back through the spacer, crimp, ring and spacer. Pull wire tightly towards spacer and crimp.

9 Add moon charm to the split ring for a finishing touch.

fire art-deco
revival necklace

SOULFUL

"Every artist dips his brush in his own soul, and paints his own nature into his pictures."
— *Henry Ward Beecher (1813 – 1887)*

Designer: Jeanne Holland

Finished Size: 16½", without clasp

Expense: $25 - $50

Level of Expertise: Intermediate

Time to Complete: More than one day

supplies

Focal stone: Vintage 25 mm x 12 mm opaque red-and-black art glass cabochon

7 opaque 4 mm red faceted rounds

6 red 6 mm round miracle beads

2 orange 8 mm rounds

2 citrine 6 mm rounds

4 citrine 7 mm ovals

2 carnelian 14 mm ovals

2 orange 8 mm baroque beads

2 orange-and-brown 12 mm baroque beads

2 amber foil 11/0 seed beads

4 opaque orange 11/0 seed beads

2 orange 12 mm disks

8 brown satin glass 11 mm bugles

6 orange 12 mm transparent diamond-shapes

26 brass bead caps, assorted*

4 fleur-de-lis drops*

1 brass Art Deco stamping, openwork, 25 mm x 18 mm stone setting*

1 brass filigree bead*

1 brass filigree classic clasp*

12" brass 3 mm cable chain*

12" brass 2 mm rolo chain*

6" brass 4 mm ladder chain*

38 brass 1½" eye pins*

6 brass 1½" head pins*

56 brass 4 mm jump rings*

2 ornate brass-end strand connectors*

*Karmul Studios, see Resources, page 160.

tool box

Needle nose pliers

Basic utility pliers

Wire cutters

how to wrap a contemporary stone with a filigree bead setting

1 Lay out the various components needed.

2 Open the filigree wrap.

3 Turn in the ends of the filigree with your needle nose pliers. Set stone inside loose setting.

4 Bend the filigree down around the stone to secure the stone in the setting. Attach jump rings in top for pendant hanger.

BEADS 50

how to create basic settings

Step-by-Step

1 Choose your filigree. The filigree must be large enough to wrap around and secure the pronged setting.

2 Bend the edges of the filigree in the exact shape of the pronged setting using your pliers (choose which ones give you the best hold on the filigree).

3 Set your stone (see below) inside the filigree setting (you may have to lift a couple of the edges to fit it in). Secure it by symmetrically tightening down the edges against the stone. This will take practice. Be sure to have plenty of filigrees on hand while in the learning stages. Leave adequate room to insert a jump ring for hanging. The filigree will not scratch the stone; however, take care to avoid marring the stone with the pliers.

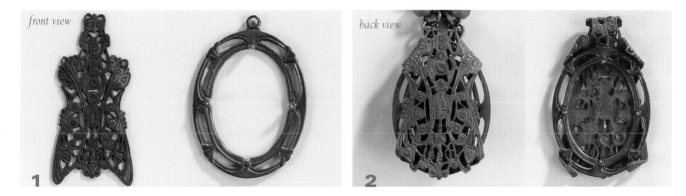

front view

back view

1

2

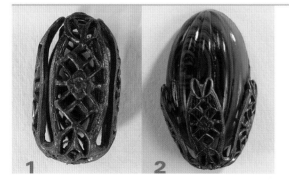

1

2

how to create the stone setting

Begin with basic settings and work your way up to advanced settings such as this. Once you have mastered the basic technique, then you are ready to create a layered setting.

1 Be sure to have all of your stones and brass pieces ready for layering.

2 Open the filigree bead and wrap it around the stone as in example, paying close attention to symmetry.

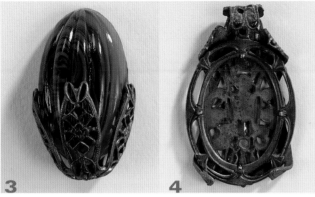

3 Place the wrapped stone in the setting. Once the stone is inside the setting, secure by symmetrically tightening down the prongs against the wrapped stone.

4 Bend the edges of the base filigree in the approximate shape of the setting using your needle nose pliers.

5 Place the set stone on top of the base filigree and tighten the base filigree around the setting. Be sure not to mark up the brass as you gently crimp down. Choose the pliers that will best help you achieve this goal.

how to create beaded chain lengths

1 Cut chain to the desired lengths.

2 Arrange beads in order of desired jewelry design.

3 Slide the non-looped end of the eye pin through the center of the bead opening. If using bead caps, slide the non-looped end of the eye pin through the bead cap with cupped end facing the bead. Hold the looped end of the eye pin firmly to the bead. Using a pair of needle nose pliers, make a loop with the non-looped end of the eye pin making it as tight as possible. Proceed to the next bead until all beads are looped on their eye pins.

4 Using pliers, attach the completed beads to each other, the pendant loop(s) or the chain with jump rings.

5 Attach the pendant to the beaded strands and the chain length using a jump ring technique.

6 Attach the clasp to the remaining bead end loops or chain with the jump rings.

artesian willow
pond necklace

ILLUMINATING

"Human subtlety will never devise an invention more beautiful, more simple or more direct than does nature, because in her inventions nothing is lacking, and nothing is superfluous." — *Leonardo da Vinci*

Designer: Wendy Mullane

Finished Size: 20", without pendant; pendant, 1⅝"

Expense: $50 or more

Level of Expertise: Intermediate

Time to Complete: One week

supplies

Focal Stones:

1 aventurine 40 mm disk

1 vintage 25 mm x18 mm art glass amber mica fleck cabochon

2 teal mottled 10 mm glass rounds

2 semi-precious gold stone 8 mm rounds

2 amber glass silver foil 10 mm rounds

2 turquoise mottled 10 mm art glass rounds

2 olive 7 mm glass swirl rounds

4 light yellow mottled 7 mm art glass rounds

2 semi-precious red poppy jasper 7 mm rounds

2 light green genuine sea pearl 6 mm faceted rounds

2 luster 4 mm glass rounds

2 vintage genuine cherry amber 6 mm faceted rounds

2 vintage turquoise 8 mm art glass ovals

2 vintage light olive swirl 10 mm art glass ovals

2 turquoise-and-amber 8 mm art glass faceted ovals

2 vintage turquoise-and-amber 20 mm striated art glass ovals

2 vintage red swirl 10 mm art glass ovals

2 vintage olive 7 mm crackle glass ovals

2 tortoise glass 8 mm faceted teardrops

2 vintage red satin glass 10 mm baroque beads

2 vintage striped olivine 13 mm baroque beads

2 vintage light green swirl 15 mm baroque beads

4 amber foil 8/0 seed beads

2 semi-precious moss agate 10 mm disks

2 dark tortoise 5 mm faceted cathedral beads

1 brass filigree classic clasp*

24" brass 3 mm cable chain*

Brass settings:

    1 moth stamping*

    2 Art Deco stampings*

    Open work 25 mm x 18 mm stone setting*

*Karmul Studios, see Resources, page 160

tool box

Needle nose pliers

Basic utility pliers

Wire cutters

2 part epoxy glue *optional

This unique Art Deco multi-layered filigree setting is encasing an exquisite vintage art glass cabochon in radiant hues of ambers and splashes of mica fleck. This mélange of brass encases a large genuine aventurine stone. A harvest of reflective beads accent the stunning center piece including: vintage and contemporary art glass, vintage and contemporary faceted glass, semi-precious gold stone, vintage genuine cherry amber and genuine sea pearls.

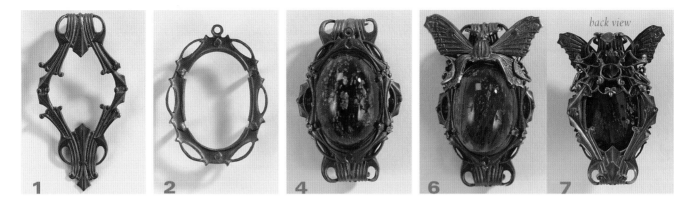

1   **2**   **4**   **6**   *back view*   **7**

5

Step-by-Step

1 Begin with the bottom base filigree. Bend the edges of the base filigree in the approximate shape of the aventurine disc bead using your needle nose pliers.

2 Set your cabochon stone inside the top filigree to check for size. This will have to be adjusted fairly often as you go. Remove the cabochon and set it aside.

3 Once the ends have been bent to hold the stone, bend up the outside prongs of the bottom base filigree to hold setting. All four prongs need to be bent upwards. Use the utility pliers for this bend.

4 Place top filigree on top of the bottom base filigree and crimp down the four prongs you just bent upwards to secure setting in place.

5 Place the cabochon in the new layered setting and tighten down the four prongs to hold the stone in place.

6 Place the Art Deco moth brass piece at the top of the art glass cabochon and bend the wings around it for a smooth fit. This will take quite a few bends with your needle nose pliers.

7 Once the moth fits, but is not yet secure, wrap the moth antennae from the back to fit around the upper part of the base filigree at the top of the setting. This will secure the top portion of the moth. Set aside.

8 Bend the edges of the moth antennae around the moth wings at the bottom to secure.

9 Slip the filigree ends around the bottom wings of the moth and crimp down until secure. Be sure not to mark up the brass as you are gently crimping down. Choose the pliers that will best help you achieve this goal.

10 Now that the setting is complete, slide it over the aventurine disc bead stone.

11 Once the aventurine is inside the filigree, secure the filigree by symmetrically tightening down the edges against the stone.

how to attach the necklace and filigree embellishments to the clasp

1 Individual unattached parts.

2 Open jump ring on clasp.

3 Slide jump ring through embellishment and close to secure. See finished side or clasp.

For creating beaded chain lengths, see instructions on page 52.

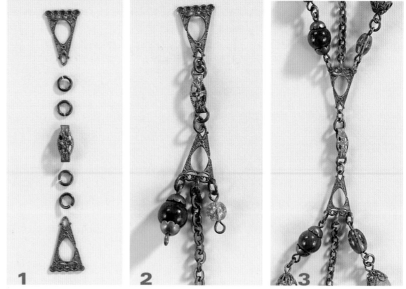

Clay/Polymer

*"And forget not that the earth
delights to feel your bare feet and
the winds long to play with your
hair."* —Kahlil Gibran

washing stones wish necklace

STRENGTH

I am not bound for any public place, but for ground of my own where I have planted vines and orchard trees, and in the heat of the day climbed up into the healing shadow of the woods. — Wendell Berry

Designer: Susan Ray

Finished Size: 32", without dangling pendant or clasp. Pendant drops: 5"

Expense: Less than $50

Level of Expertise: Intermediate

Time to Complete: One week

to make beads

supplies

½ pkg. (1 ounce) alizarin crimson PREMO! by Polyform,

½ pkg. (1 ounce) purple PREMO! by Polyform

½ pkg. (1 ounce) black PREMO! by Polyform

½ pkg. (1 ounce) ecru PREMO! by Polyform

¼ pkg. (½ ounce) burnt umber PREMO! by Polyform

1 pkg. (2 ounces) black Granitex by Polyform

⅓ sheet of gold and orange or copper gold leaf

1 bottle bronze Susan Jones' Jones Tones Micro-Cut Glitter

1 pkg. Darice Charming Embellishments

1 roll brass 20-gauge wire

tool box

6 large wooden skewers (for crafting only, do not bake clay on the skewer)

Pasta machine (dedicated to polymer clay)

Toaster oven (dedicated to polymer clay)

Acrylic rolling pin

Clay cutter

Wire cutters

Large, fine emery board

Clean, dry work surface

Step-by-Step

1 Condition all clay following manufacturer's directions. Create lengths of clay approximately 2" wide on the thickest setting of the pasta machine.

2 Create four skewers of clay from one package of PREMO! Granitex clay. *See Susan Ray's Basic Skewer Beads Instructions, page 137.* Set aside.

3 Create MEDIUM slabs 2" x 3" lengths of each: alizarin crimson, purple, ecru, burnt umber and black on middle setting of the pasta machine.

4 Create four styles of cane using the following method: Lay alternating medium slabs together on top of each other. Use two to three color combinations. Cut away excess clay from edges. Roll in a jellyroll fashion. These will become some of your canes.

5 Set the canes aside to rest. Keep any remaining canes in a sealed plastic storage container for use in another project.

6 After you have completed your canes, tear the remaining clay slabs into approximately ½" pieces. Avoid uniformity. In this instance, the clay pieces should be odd shapes and sizes.

7 Apply odd pieces of different clay colors, the gold leaf, and very thin slices of the canes to the skewers to create interesting patterns. Roll smooth between applications. Your clay should "grow" to fill the entire length of each skewer as you add additional canes and clay pieces. When you are satisfied with your design, allow the skewered clay to rest for at least one hour before cutting.

helpful tips: *You can make some unusual canes by combining two or more jellyrolls. Simply press the jellyrolls together lengthwise. Apply a slab of complementary clay around them. Roll altogether until you have a new, smooth jellyroll. Cut thin slices starting at one end.*

make the twisted beads

1 Holding one skewer, start at one end of the skewer and twist the clay in a barber shop pole fashion until you reach the other end. Continue to twist until the surface begins to rise and you are happy with the striped pattern. Be careful not to weaken the thickness of the bead wall by twisting the clay too tightly. Allow to rest for at least one hour.

cut the beads

NOTE: Clay cutters are very sharp! Be sure you always pick up your clay cutter properly. Follow manufacturer's directions.

1 Skewer size 1 (TWISTED clay) - Cut six 1¼" twisted beads. Tap ends to smooth.

2 Skewer size 2 - Cut eight ¾" beads and roll in the palm of your hands to create seven 16 mm rounds and one 14 mm x 12 mm oval. If you lose some of your design while rolling, reapply a thin slice of your cane to cover. Roll until smooth. Pierce with the end of your skewer to make center holes for stringing.

NOTE: Use a small skewer or hatpin to create holes of different sizes, dependent upon the stringing materials you choose to use.

3 Skewer size 3 - Cut four 1" beads resembling barrels. Tap ends to smooth. Cut two 1½" beads. Remove each 1½" bead

to a separate skewer. Place on your work surface. Using your forefingers, roll each end of each bead applying slight pressure. Before long the bead ends will begin to taper. When your tapered ends are uniform, cut away outside edges to clean up the ends. Tap ends to smooth. Now you have two tapered beads. This technique takes additional time but the look is definitely worth it.

4 Skewer size 4 - Cut six ½" beads and roll in the palm of your hands to create six 12 mm rounds. Use a small skewer or hatpin to make holes for stringing. Cut one 1½" bead and one 1¾" bead. The 1½" bead will become the 32 mm x 6 mm pendant and the 1¾" bead will become the 34 mm x 8 mm pendant form. Set beads aside on the toaster-oven baking pan until you complete the pendants.

make the pendants

1 Cut 1½" and 1¾" beads open lengthwise. Roll through pasta machine on one of the thinner settings to increase the mass. Lay flat. Make a tiny ball (the size of a pea) of scrap clay. Apply the flattened clay over the scrap ball. Cut away excess ends. Roll into a new ball in the palm of your hands until all the seams disappear. Once satisfied with the design, press the ball firmly in the palm of your hand or on work surface to create a disk. (You may want to use a sheet of vellum paper on your work surface to easily pick up new pendant without disturbing its shape.) Each disk will become one of the pendants. Choose two wishes from the Darice Charming Embellishments. Press the wishes into the center of each pendant.

You can find some of the most interesting items to insert into your clay in some very unusual places! Try dog tags, coins, or old earring fronts, or even discarded pendants from old costume jewelry.

2 Cut five ¼" pieces of 20-gauge wire. Create U-shaped wire by folding in half over the middle of a wooden skewer. Insert U-shapes into the pendants. The first pendant has one "U" at the top and three at the bottom. The second pendant has one "U" at the top.

3 Place remaining beads and pendant on toaster-oven baking pan. Bake all following manufacturer's directions and allow to cool completely before removing from oven.

4 Use a large, fine emery board to smooth all sides of beads. (Be careful not to apply too much pressure over foiled areas. The foil can be sanded away.) Wipe clean.

stringing the necklace

supplies

7 polymer ¾" round beads

6 polymer ½" round beads

2 polymer 1½" tapered beads

4 polymer 1" barrel beads

6 polymer 1¼" twisted beads

1 polymer 14 mm x 12 mm oval

1 HOPE 1¾" diameter pendant

1 WISH 1½" diameter pendant

15 AB luster caramel 6/0 glass beads

46 AB amethyst 6/0 gold foil Miyuki triangles

24 iris-brown 8 mm potato pearls

4 multi-faceted 10 mm diameter crystals

2 multi-faceted 8 mm diameter crystals

6 copper bicone 6 mm metal spacers

26 Delica root beer beads (24 to create loop for center dangle and 2 to act as stops for dangles)

2 gold 4" head pins

1 toggle clasp set

36" of 7-strand .018 mm gauge flexible wire (for stringing necklace)

27" of 7-strand .018 mm gauge flexible wire (for creating dangles for the second pendant)

2 brass 2 mm x 3 mm crimp beads (for stringing necklace)

4 brass crimp beads (for creating dangles for the second pendant)

1 roll 20-gauge brass wire

tool box

Flat nose pliers

Needle nose pliers

Wire cutters

Hemostat

Crimping pliers

Step-by-Step

See Susan Ray's Basic Skewer Beads, page 137.

See Basic Instructions, Single-Strand Necklace, page 146.

1 Crimp one end of your toggle onto the 36" piece of flexible wire.

2 String one half of your beads according to photo.

3 String on pendant and the remaining beads.

4 Using a brass crimp bead, complete by attaching the other end of your toggle clasp.

5 Dangles: *See Dangles in Basic Stringing Instructions, page 154, for other methods of attachment.* Cut three 9" pieces from the 27" wire for dangles. String a crimp bead onto each 9" wire and create a loop by bringing the short tail of wire back through the crimp bead. Use your flat nose pliers to crimp in place.

6 Create the two short dangles: String all beads and a crimp bead onto the wire. String one Delica. Make a loop back through the crimp bead, carefully avoiding the Delica. This will allow the Delica to act as a stop. String the wire through the Miyuki bead and crimp in place. Cut excess wire.

7 Create the center dangle: String all beads and two crimps (one on each end) of your wire. Attach a hemostat to one end. Create an open loop by stringing 12 Delicas onto the other end of the flexible wire. Slip the loop through the center "U" of the pendant and back through the crimp bead and the caramel 6/0. Crimp. Cut away excess wire.

NOTE: Check to be sure your loops are crimped properly.

8 Remove hemostat: To attach the other end of this dangle to the second pendant, string 12 Delica beads onto wire. Slip the loop through the "U" of the second pendant and back through the crimp bead and caramel 6/0 bead. Crimp in place. Cut excess wire.

9 Make a WISH!

fossilized slate brooch and earrings

NATURAL

"Study nature, love nature, stay close to nature. It will never fail you."
—*Frank Lloyd Wright (1868 - 1959)*

Designer: Patty Kimle

Finished Size: Pin, 2¾" x 2¼"; earrings, 1¾" x 1"

Expense: Less than $20

Level of Expertise: Beginner

Time to Complete: One day

supplies

1 pkg. (2 ounces) black Sculpey PREMO! polymer clay

1 decorative skeletal leaf

8" square of waxed paper

Gel formula cyano-acrylate glue (Super Glue)

1" pin back

1 pair earring posts with 8 mm pad

Black and white acrylic paint

tool box

Pasta machine (dedicated to polymer clay)

Paper towel

Acrylic roller

Oven or toaster oven (dedicated to polymer clay)

Small paintbrush

1 Condition the black clay by rolling it through the pasta machine following manufacturer's directions until a smooth sheet is formed. Roll clay to approximately 1 mm thickness. Lay the sheet on a piece of white paper, allowing to rest and return to room temperature. The clay must be cool to tear easily. If it is warm, it will stretch instead of tear.

2 For the pin: Tear the sheet into three strips and randomly lay each strip over each other with the narrowest piece on top. Roll gently with the acrylic roller to slightly compress the stack. If desired, damage the leaf a little bit by tearing at the edges. Lay the leaf on the clay and roll to impress the pattern into the surface. Carefully remove the leaf. Crumple the waxed paper and smooth it out again. Roll this sheet onto the surface of the clay. Trim two sides of the stack to the desired shape. Press pin back into the back of the stack. Bake according to the manufacturer's recommendations. Allow to cool.

3 Repeat Step 2 with two layers of clay and cut into desired shapes for earrings.

4 When cool, mix approximately one quarter teaspoon each of the black and white acrylic paints to comprise a light grey color. Apply the paint over the entire surface of the pin and earrings. Allow to dry only slightly. Remove most of the paint with a damp paper towel. Remove the pin back and glue it in place with Super Glue. Glue the earring posts in place.

Polymer clay might be called the "Great Imitator" because it is so wonderful for many faux effects, including the imitation of natural materials, stones, metals, and more. This project quite simply, yet effectively, imitates slate. A slightly damaged paper leaf adds a bit of mystery, drama and the allusion of time.

over the rainbow lanyard necklace and bracelet set

INTRINSIC

"In all things of nature there is something of the marvelous."
— Aristotle (384 BC - 322 BC), Parts of Animals

Designer: Marie Segal

Finished Size: Necklace: 18"; Bracelet: 8"

Expense: Less than $50

Level of Expertise: Intermediate

Time to Complete: One week

supplies for necklace and bracelet

18" roll of 16-gauge black artistic wire

3 ounces pearl PREMO!

3 ounces white Super Flex

½ ounce red pearl PREMO!

1 ounce red Super Flex

1 ounce gold PREMO!

½ ounce yellow Super Flex

½ ounce green Super Flex

½ ounce pearl green PREMO!

½ ounce blue Super Flex

1 ounce blue pearl PREMO!

½ ounce orange Super Flex

tool box

Side cutters

Chain nose pliers

Round nose pliers

Cookie sheet (dedicated to polymer clay)

Quick-dry glue, such as Hot Stuff (from the Clay Factory, see Resources, page 160)

Needle tool or large darning needle

Pencil or ⅜" piece of tubing, like brass or metal

Sculpey Super Slicer

Flat nose pliers

how to mix the "Over the Rainbow" color set

Both the bracelet and the necklace are made the same way.

Red: ¼ block of pearl PREMO! to ¼ block of white Super Flex, plus ¼ block red pearl PREMO! to ¼ block red Super Flex.

Orange: ¼ block of pearl PREMO! to ¼ block white Super Flex, plus ¼ block of gold PREMO! to ¼ block of orange Super Flex.

Yellow: ¼ block of pearl PREMO! to ¼ block of white Super Flex, plus ¼ block of gold PREMO! to ¼ block of yellow Super Flex.

Green: ¼ block of pearl PREMO! to ¼ block of white Super Flex, plus ¼ block of pearl green PREMO! to ¼ block of green Super Flex.

Blue: ¼ block of pearl PREMO! to ¼ block of white Super Flex, plus ¼ block of blue pearl PREMO! to ¼ block of blue Super Flex.

Purple: ¼ block of pearl PREMO! to ¼ block of white Super Flex, plus ¼ block of blue pearl PREMO! to ¼ block of red Super Flex.

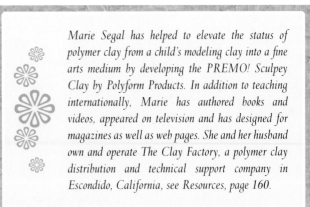

Marie Segal has helped to elevate the status of polymer clay from a child's modeling clay into a fine arts medium by developing the PREMO! Sculpey Clay by Polyform Products. In addition to teaching internationally, Marie has authored books and videos, appeared on television and has designed for magazines as well as web pages. She and her husband own and operate The Clay Factory, a polymer clay distribution and technical support company in Escondido, California, see Resources, page 160.

how to extrude and bake the clay cords

The general rule of thumb for making the clay mixture is: 1 part Super Flex to 1 part PREMO! Sculpey. (I keep my batches to 2 ounces.) Start with ½ block of the flex clay and squeeze together until it starts to soften.

NOTE: If you roll it through the pasta machine or in your hands, it will want to break apart. Keep squeezing until it starts to stick together. You will notice the difference in consistency. When it is nice and smooth, flatten into a pancake about ½" thick.

extruding clay tools and supplies

Your clay color set

Kemper EZ- Squeeze Klay Gun adaptor (Clay Factory)

Kemper Klay Gun (Clay Factory)

Largest flat strip disk in set of disks that comes with the clay gun

Cool Tool knife end (Clay Factory)

Step-by-Step

1 Condition ½ block of PREMO! Sculpey and mix with each color from page 66, until one color. After you have mixed up the complete set, flatten out the clay colors so they are about ½" thick. Stack the colors on top of each other and cut into ½" sections.

2 Peel the separate colors apart and roll the first color into a coil slightly smaller than the Klay Gun barrel. Then roll another color.

3 Add second color by smashing the ends together. Try not to trap air between the colors, as this will form an air bubble in the cord. Roll both colors into a new coil, smoothing the seam at the junction of the colors. Insert into the Klay Gun barrel all the way to the end.

4 Place the nut with the disk on the end and place into the adaptor. Run the plunger into the Klay Gun barrel by squeezing the handle. Extrude out the strip into a little pile. Do not compact. Place on surface or cookie sheet.

5 Pull back the plunger from the Klay gun and remove the extruder. Take off the nut and disk from the end, and with the "Cool Tool" knife end, remove all the excess clay from inside the Klay Gun barrel. Gather the excess and roll into a little coil. Continue to the next coil colors in line. Load the gun and put the disk and nut together again and squeeze out the next color, cleaning out the gun each time.

4

note of caution

I find if I leave the clay in the Klay Gun, and just add more, I get what I call "blow outs" in the cord. — Marie Segal

5

6 When your entire tray is filled with little piles, preheat the oven to 350 degrees.

7 Bake according to manufacturer's directions in roasting pan or dedicated toaster oven.

Roasting pans only: If desired, get a roasting pan with a lid to bake your clay cords. Bake your cords at 350 degrees for 10 minutes, then shut off the oven, and let cool in the oven. Don't open the door until it is well cooled, about an hour or two. Be sure to follow manufacturer's directions explicitly.

6

form your lanyard

Step-by-Step

1 Stretch out two of the little piles of cord. Find the center of each one and force the end of the needle tool through the center of each flattened cord. Leave the cord on the needle tool until you get the wire turned for the bracelet.

2 Make the loop for the bracelet: At one end of the wire, bend the end 2" at a right angle with your round nose pliers. With the round nose pliers, create a wrapped loop. Cut off the excess wire with your side cutters and flatten the cut edge against the bottom wire. *(See Wrapped Loop Method, page 152.)*

3 Take your loop off the pencil and thread the end of the wire through the holes you made in the center of the cords. Spread the cords so they form a cross at a 45-degree angle.

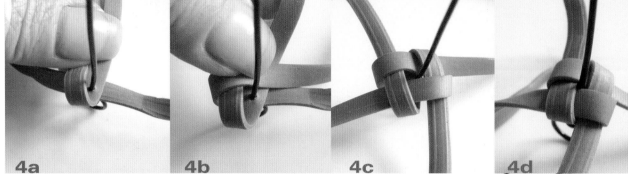

4a **4b** **4c** **4d**

4e

4 Create the box pattern of a basic lanyard: Fold cord in half. Start with one cord and fold it over the next, moving in a clockwise direction. Fold the next cord over the first. Fold the next cord in line over the previous.

5 The end of the last cord will be threaded under the loop on the first one, locking it into place. Pull the ends tight to form what looks like a block. This will create a box stitch. Repeat in a counterclockwise direction.

6 Start with one cord and fold it back over the last layer you made. Take the next cord in line and fold it over the first.

7 Fold the next cord in line over the last and thread the end of the last cord through and under the first cord, locking it into place. Pull all of the cords tight. Proceed counterclockwise until you have reached the desired length. *(See Gluing on Additional Cord for more information, page 71.)*

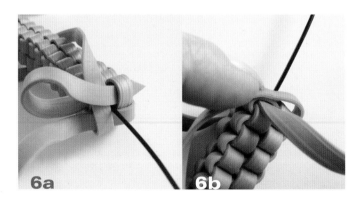

6a **6b**

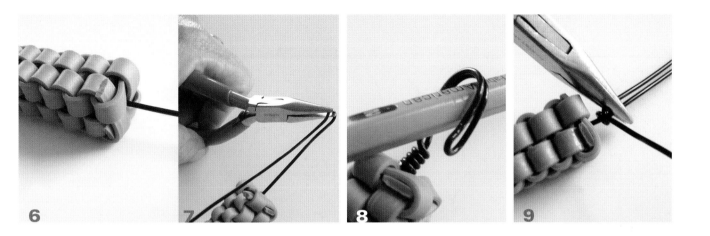

gluing on additional cord

The small piles you made when you extruded the cord aren't long enough to complete your bracelet and necklace. When the cords you are weaving get down to about 5", you are going to have to "glue on" more cord.

Step-by-Step

1 Slice your clay at an angle on the end of the cord.

2 Choose and add another cord pile. Cut it in half, cutting one of the ends with your blade at an angle. The more surface area you make by cutting at an angle, the stronger the bond will be where the cords join, and the more surface area the glue will adhere to.

3 Put a small amount of the quick-dry glue on one of the angle cuts and adhere it to the other. Hold it there for a little while to give it enough time to grab. Let these joins dry for 5 minutes before proceeding with the weaving.

4 Continue as if you are going to braid another level of the box cord and fold over the first cord. Place a small amount of glue on the cording under it. Hold it there until it sets. Do not pull it completely flat or you will have a hard time threading the last cord under it. Do not leave it too loose either, or it will be too big of loop when you are finished.

5 Fold the next cord over the first, and glue it in place. Fold over the next and glue as before.

6 Cut the end of the last cord into a point and thread through the first loop. Pull it firmly through and back. Place glue into the space between the cord under it. Place a little glue inside as far as you can get it and hold it down. When the glue has set, leave it for at least 10 minutes. Trim off the excess cording with your clay-slicing blade. Be very careful not to cut into the cord underneath.

7 Grab the wire about 1½" above the finished end and bend it in half so the wire is doubled. About ¼" from the finished braid, bend the end of the bent wire at a 45-degree angle. Grab the two wires over the 45-degree bend, and pull the tail of the wire around the center wire, above the braid end. Wind the wire tightly around the center wire, down to the braided end.

8 Cut off the excess with your side cutters, and flatten the end of the wire against the center wire. This should be a very tight fit against the braided end. Bend the doubled end of the wire over your pencil and make a hook.

9 With your flat nose pliers, bend the small loop up. The hook will fit in the loop at the other end to form the closure for the bracelet.

make the end caps

supplies

Kemper cutters: Round: ⅝" and ³⁄₁₆"; Teardrop: ⁵⁄₁₆"

1 to 2 ounce block each ecru and white PREMO! Sculpey

Pasta machine or roller (dedicated to polymer clay)

"Cool Tool" knife end and ball stylus end

Black acrylic paint

¼" round stencil brush

Paper towel

Step-by-Step

1 Mix ¼ block of ecru clay with ¼ block of white clay until they are one color.

2 Roll out your mixed clay on the thickest setting of the pasta machine.

3 Cut out the following with the round Kemper cutter: two ⅝" circles, eight ⁵⁄₁₆" teardrops and two ³⁄₁₆" rounds.

4 Place the teardrops onto the circle in a cross pattern. I start at one quarter of the circle and apply the rest, one after the other, in a clockwise motion.

5 Mark the center veins in the teardrop with the knife end of the "Cool Tool." To mark the side veins of the leaf with the teardrop cutter, place the point into the center vein, and pull back and down towards you. Do not pull down until the cutting edge of the cutter is horizontal or you will cut too deep.

6 Place the little balls that you rolled from the ³⁄₁₆" cutter into the center of the leaves where they all meet. Poke the ball stylus end of the "Cool Tool," through the center of the ball, down to the work surface, making a hole to accept the wire from the necklace and the bracelet.

7 Bake in a preheated 275-degree oven for 25 minutes following manufacturer's directions.

8 Let cool completely before antiquing.

9 With the dry stencil brush, rub the black paint into the surface of the end caps. Rub off the excess from the pieces with damp, not drippy, paper towel.

10 String one end cap before beginning. Proceed with braiding, then string on the second end cap before finishing.

rain forest man necklace

REFLECTION

"If winter is slumber and spring is birth, and summer is life, then autumn rounds out to be reflection. It's a time of year when the leaves are down and the harvest is in and the perennials are gone. Mother Earth just closed up the drapes on another year and it's time to reflect on what's come before." — Mitchell Burgess, Northern Exposure, Thanksgiving, 1992

Designer: Tracy Callahan

Finished Size: 32", without dangling pendant or clasp. Pendant drops: 5"

Expense: Less than $50

Level of Expertise: Intermediate

Time to Complete: One week

2 pkg. (2 ounces each) black polymer clay

Small amounts each color PearlEx Powders: duo blue-green, spring green, Aztec gold, interference violet, duo red-blue

Your choice of texture sheet or rubber stamps

Krylon webbing spray: white and black

1 skein each of metallic thread: purple, turquoise

18" to 20" Buna cord

2 vitrail 12 mm rounds (with holes large enough to accommodate the Buna cord)

2 vitrail 8 mm rounds (with holes large enough to accommodate the Buna cord)

1 barrel clasp

Mask/face mold

Cyano-acrylate gel glue (any brand)

Sealer (any type)

tool box

Needle tool

1" Kemper square cutters

Circle cutter

Pasta machine (dedicated to polymer clay)

Newspaper

Toaster oven (dedicated to polymer clay)

Spray bottle with water

1-6

10

Step-by-Step

1 Condition black polymer clay using the pasta machine. Roll out a sheet on the thickest setting of your pasta machine.

2 Spray your texture sheet with water and press into your clay sheet.

3 Randomly spread the PearlEx powder colors (duo blue-green, spring green, interference violet, and duo red-blue) in different areas on the textured clay. Use the Aztec gold to highlight certain spots.

4 Cut 12 to 14 squares using the Kemper square cutters. Use the needle tool and poke a hole through one corner of each square. Set aside.

5 Use large circle cutter to cut out the medallion. Mostly duo red-blue and interference violet PearlEx powders were used on this project with Aztec gold placed around the edges.

6 Press some black clay into the mask/face mold. Once you have the face, spread the Aztec gold PearlEx powders on it. Tack the face mold onto the medallion with a little glue.

7 Cut some odd, small shapes out of textured and colored scrap clay and place around the face.

8 Bake the pieces at 265 degrees for 20 minutes in toaster oven.

9 When the squares are cool, lay on a piece of newspaper and spray lightly with white and black webbing spray. Seal if desired.

10 Thread a needle with turquoise and purple metallic thread. Attach all the pieces on the buna cord by stitching and tying off a knot, letting some of the fiber ends hang down. You also can add a bead between each of the squares. Don't tie the squares on too tight or they will not lay right. Add barrel clasp with overhand knot. Cut away excess cord.

gecko in the leaves necklace

AUTUMN

"A woodland in full color is awesome as a forest fire, in magnitude at least, but a single tree is like a dancing tongue of flame to warm the heart." — *Hal Borland*

Designer: Tracy Callahan

Finished Size: 22", without clasp

Expense: Less than $25

Level of Expertise: Beginner/ Intermediate

Time to Complete: One day

supplies

2 pkg. (2 ounces each) black polymer clay

28" rust-color satin cording

2 sterling silver 6 mm spring rings

2 charm holders

Luna Lights paint: dark blue, copper, gold, yellow, maroon

PearlEx powders: blue, green, gold

Polymer clay sealer or Future floor wax

tool box

X-acto knife

Pasta machine (dedicated to polymer clay)

Maple leaf stamp

Small maple leaf mold

Gecko mold

Toaster oven (dedicated to polymer clay)

Small paintbrush

Cotton swab

Step-by-Step

1 Condition black polymer clay by using the pasta machine. Roll out a sheet on the thickest setting of your pasta machine.

2 Press the maple leaf stamp three times into the sheet of clay.

3 Use your X-acto knife to cut around the leaf designs. You should have three leaves.

4 Position your leaves by placing two leaves side by side and then place the third leaf on top of the other two, leaving about half of a leaf showing on both sides. Set aside.

5 Press leftover black clay into the small leaf mold. Make eight of the small leaf designs. Set aside.

6 If desired, press leftover black clay into the gecko mold. Although this step is optional, it adds a decorative element to your final project.

4

7 The large leaves are painted with copper, maroon, and gold Luna Lights paints. Two of the small leaves are painted with a mixture of blue, yellow, and gold Luna Lights paints. Use the gold as a highlight element. Use your creativity; don't be afraid to experiment.

8 Skip this step if you do not make the gecko. Apply the PearlEx powders (green, blue and gold) to the gecko. Use the gold to highlight your piece. Apply powders with fingers or cotton swab.

9 Arrange finished pieces to your liking. Bake at 265 degrees for 25 minutes in toaster oven.

10 Two tube beads were made (see Susan Ray's Skewer Beads, page 137) for the backside of the leaves to hold the satin cording. Insert the cord into the bead and then tie a knot to secure. Do the same for the other side. Add a wooden or glass bead; this is what makes the necklace adjustable. The bead hole needs to be big enough to insert both satin cords and provide a snug fit. On the end of each satin cord, tie on a spring ring, add a charm holder to the end of the leaf, and attach it to the spring ring. Repeat this for both cords.

11 Optional: Seal with suitable polymer clay sealer or Future floor wax.

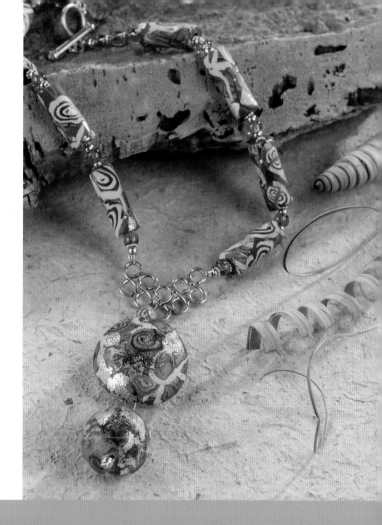

gold leaf blooms
pendant drop
necklace

PATIENT

"Adopt the pace of nature: her secret is patience." — Ralph Waldo Emerson

Designer: Susan Ray

Finished Size: 18", without dangling pendant or clasp. Pendant size: 2"

Expense: Less than $50

Level of Expertise: Beginner/ Intermediate

Time to Complete: One weekend

to make beads

supplies

1 pkg. (2 ounces) neon yellow PREMO! by Polyform

2 pkg. (2 ounces each) green PREMO! by Polyform

½ pkg. (1 ounce) cad red PREMO! by Polyform

½ pkg. (1 ounce) black Granitex by Polyform

½ pkg. (1 ounce) raw umber PREMO! by Polyform

⅓ sheet gold-and-orange gold leaf

1 bottle bronze or gold Susan Jones' Jones Tones Glitter

1 roll brass 20-gauge wire

tool box

2 large wooden skewers

Pasta machine (dedicated to polymer clay)

Toaster oven (dedicated to polymer clay)

Acrylic rolling pin

Clay cutter

Wire cutters

Clean, dry work surface

Large, fine emery board

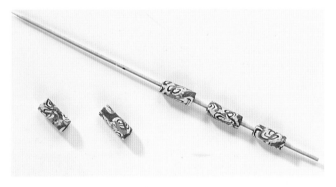

PREMO!

Neon yellow seems like a very modern color, however, used here with deep green polymer, gold leaf and gold Egyptian accents, it takes on the look of an antiquity of ethnic descent.

Step-by-Step

1 Condition all clay following manufacturer's directions, creating lengths of clay approximately 2" wide on the thickest setting of the pasta machine.

2 Create two skewers of clay from one package of green PREMO! clay. *See Susan Ray's Basic Skewer Beads Instructions, page 137.* Set aside.

3 Create three THICK slabs, 2" x 3" lengths of each: black Granitex, cad red, neon yellow and raw umber at thickest setting.

4 Create two MEDIUM slabs, 2" x 3" lengths of each: black Granitex, cad red, neon yellow and raw umber by reducing to a middle setting on your pasta machine.

5 Create four to six styles of cane using the following method: Lay the thick black Granitex on top of a thinner neon yellow clay. Cut away excess. Roll the clay in a jellyroll fashion. This will become one of your canes. Experiment! Use different thicknesses and color combinations to create three to five additional canes. Be creative! Some of my canes have three to four colors and contain two to three different dimensions! Set all aside to rest.

6 After you have completed your canes, tear the remaining clay slabs into approximately ½" pieces. Avoid uniformity. In this instance, the clay pieces should be odd shapes and sizes.

7 Apply odd pieces of different clay colors, the gold leaf and very thin slices of the canes to the skewers with clay base to create interesting patterns. Roll smooth.

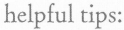
helpful tips:

You can make some unusual canes by combining two or more jellyrolls. Simply press the jellyrolls together lengthwise. Apply a slab of complementary clay around them. Roll all together until you have a new, smooth jellyroll. Cut thin slices starting at one end.

8 Cut the skewered clay into eight 1¼" beads, one 1" bead for dangle, one 1" bead (for pendant) and one ¼" bead for dangle. Remove from skewer. Tap ends to smooth.

9 Place eight 1¼" beads onto the toaster-oven's baking pan.

10 Cut one 1" bead open lengthwise. Roll through your pasta machine on one of the thinner settings to increase the mass. Lay flat. Make a 1½" ball of scrap clay. Apply the flattened clay over the scrap ball. Cut away excess ends. Roll into a new ball until all the seams disappear. Once you are satisfied with your design, press firmly in the palm of your hand to create a pendant.

11 Cut two ¼" pieces of 20-gauge wire. Create two "U's" by folding in half over the middle of a wooden skewer. Insert these U's into the top and bottom of the pendant.

12 Take the remaining two beads and roll into separate balls. If you lose some of your design while rolling, reapply a thin slice of your cane to cover. Roll until smooth. Pierce with the end of your skewer to make center holes. This will result in two round beads, 1" and ¼" in diameter. These beads will eventually be used as part of your pendant attachment.

13 Place remaining beads and pendant on toaster-oven baking pan. Bake following manufacturer's directions. Allow to cool completely before removing from oven.

14 Use a large, fine emery board to smooth all sides of beads. Caution not to remove gold leaf during sanding with emery board. Wipe clean.

helpful tips:

To add glitter highlights to your beads, simply apply Susan Jones' Jones Tones Micro-Cut Glitter onto your work surface. Use a toothpick to separate the glitter into rows, then roll your beads through the glitter. Bake as usual. Jones Tones glitter will not burn away in the baking and will enhance the old-world look of this piece.

necklace

supplies

8 skewer beads 1¼" length x ½" diameter

1 round polymer bead 1" diameter

1 round polymer bead ¼" diameter

1 pendant 1½" diameter

25 gold 6/0 glass beads

14 gold 8 mm glass crow beads

1 gold 6 mm faceted disk

22 gold 2 mm fluted edge spacers

1 brass 2 mm bead

2 gold 4" headpins

1 gold three-way connector

1 toggle clasp set

40" flexible wire

7 brass 2 mm x 3 mm crimp beads

tool box

Flat nose pliers

Needle nose pliers

Wire cutters

Crimping tool

Step-by-Step

See Basic Instructions, Single-Strand Necklace, page 146.

1 Cut two 15" pieces of flexible wire.

2 Attach one end of your clasp to the flexible wire using a crimp bead. String **one each** of the following beads in this sequence:

Gold 6/0 glass bead, gold crow, gold 6/0 glass bead, gold crow, gold 6/0 glass bead, gold crow, gold 6/0 glass bead, gold 2 mm spacer, skewer bead, gold 2 mm spacer, gold 6/0 glass bead, gold crow, gold 6/0 glass bead

3 Repeat the following bead sequence three more times: one gold 2 mm spacer, one 2 mm spacer, one skewer bead, one gold 6/0 glass bead, one gold crow.

4 Attach one end of connector to necklace using a brass crimp bead.

5 Repeat instructions for the other side of the necklace.

6

6 Create a dangle for below the connector using a 5" piece of flexible wire. Loop the wire around the the connector. Slide on a crimp bead, crimp bead in place. String one 4 mm gold bead, one ¼" round polymer bead, crimp bead, one 4 mm gold bead. Wrap wire through the U-shaped wire at the top of the pendant, go back through the gold bead, crimp bead and polymer bead. Secure the crimp bead and cut away excess wire.

7 Assemble the ball for the lower portion of the pendant: Cut a 5" piece of flexible wire and fold in half. Loop wire around bottom U-shaped pin on disk pendant. String the following on the double wire: One 2 mm brass bead, one gold 6 mm faceted disk, one 1" round polymer bead, crimp bead, one gold 6/0 glass bead and one crimp bead. Crimp the bead under the polymer bead. Apply Super Glue under last crimp bead and crimp in place. Cut away excess wire.

 tip *Extra crimp beads strengthen the hold for heavier pendants. They also can be used as a decorative element.*

florentine memories earrings

WONDER

"Earth and sky, woods and fields, lakes and rivers, the mountain and the sea, are excellent schoolmasters, and teach some of us more than we can ever learn from books."
— *John Lubbock, Sr.*

Designer: syndee holt

Finished Size: 2½"

Expense: Less than $50

Level of Expertise: All

Time to Complete: One day

supplies

2 ounces copper PREMO! Sculpey

Sculpey Texture Sheets – I used Hide and Seek Squares

Gold PearlEx stamp pad

Jacquard PearlEx and other stamp pads

Pearl Ex interference blue and interference violet stamp pads

Pearl Ex super copper powder, just a dab

Future floor wax, Sculpey Glaze, or Flecto varathane (brush-type, not spray)

4" of 16-gauge copper artistic wire, for loops

Ear wires

tool box

Pasta machine (dedicated to polymer clay)

Index cards

Acrylic clay roller or wooden roller

Bamboo skewer

Sculpey Super Slicer

Pencil

Step-by-Step

1 Roll out a sheet of copper clay on the widest setting on your pasta machine and place the sheet on an index card. The clay should be about 2½" wide x 6" long.

2 Select the portion of the texture sheet you wish to use for your earrings. Ink that portion of the texture sheet and lay it on the clay. Applying medium pressure, use your roller to emboss the stamp into the clay.

3 Carefully remove the stamp from the clay. Pick up the index card and peel the clay from the card. Put the clay back on the card and set on your work surface.

When I make earrings, I generally make three pieces. That way I can pick the best of the three to create the final set! — syndee holt

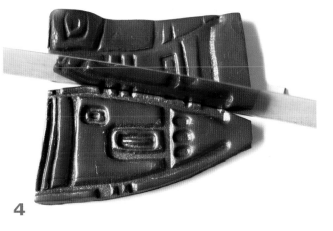

4

4 Use your Super Slicer to trim the clay to the area you selected. The blade will bend easily to cut curves.

5 Gently swipe the surface of the clay with both the interference blue and interference violet stamp pads, adding touches of random color.

6 Dip the tip of your finger into the super copper Pearl Ex and randomly daub it onto the surface over the inks. This copper highlight should not be a complete covering of the surface.

7 Use the back of your bamboo skewer to create the hole for hanging your earrings on the ear wires.

8 Put the finished pieces on the index card. Place on your baking tray and bake as directed on the clay package.

9 When the clay has cooled, seal the surface with a very light coat of Future floor wax.

10 Attach the clay to the wires. Create wire loops by winding the wire around a pencil. Use wire cutters to cut off each loop.

Store your PearlEx powders with the lid down so when the lid is removed there is enough PearlEx remaining in the lid to work with the clay. — syndee holt

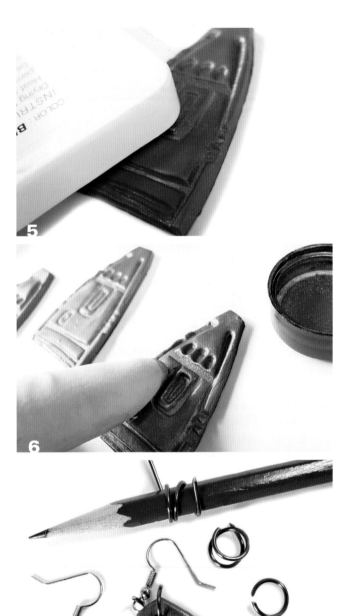

robin's egg necklace

FRAGILE

"Nature will bear the closest inspection. She invites us to lay our eye level with her smallest leaf, and take an insect view of its plane." — Henry David Thoreau

Designer: Susan Ray

Finished Size: 24", without dangling pendant and clasp. Pendant size: 2"

Expense: Less than $50

Level of Expertise: Intermediate

Time to Complete: One weekend

make the beads

supplies to make the eggs

½ pkg. (1 ounce) PREMO! in the following colors: raw umber, turquoise, pearl white, burnt umber, ecru

½ ounce black PREMO! to create 1" size balls, each color and quantity as follows: 3 black, 4 pearl white , 3 raw umber, 1 turquoise, 1 ecru

¼ pkg. (½ ounce) of black Granitex (conditioned and cut into 6 pieces)

Flat white acrylic craft paint.

Craft paintbrush and container for water

supplies for secondary beads

¼ pkg. (½ ounce) ecru PREMO!

¼ pkg. (½ ounce) raw umber PREMO!

¼ pkg. (½ ounce) pearl white PREMO!

¼ pkg. (½) ounce black Granitex

supplies for nest pendant

¼ pkg. (½) ounce raw umber PREMO!

¼ pkg. (½) ounce black PREMO!

2" of 22-gauge silver wire

supplies for mini eggs

¼ pkg. (½ ounce) black Granitex (cut into 3 pieces)

Plus, pea size balls of raw umber, ecru, pearl white, black or turquoise

optional

White pepper

Black pepper

Instant coffee grounds

tool box

1 silver 5" hatpin

3 large wooden skewers

Pasta machine (dedicated to polymer clay)

Toaster oven (dedicated to polymer clay)

Acrylic rolling pin

Fine emery board

Clay cutter

Clean, dry work surface

Step-by-Step

create the polymer color mixes for each egg

1 Condition all clay following manufacturer's directions by rolling each color through a pasta machine.

2 Create the brown egg: Mix 1" balls of pearl white and black with a 1" ball of raw umber, then mix one of the six pieces of black Granitex to this mixture until well blended. Set aside.

3 Create the turquoise egg: Mix one 1" ball of pearl white with a 1" ball of turquoise, then mix one of the six pieces of black Granitex to this mixture until well blended. Set aside.

4 Create the beige egg: Mix 1" ball of black with 1" ball of raw umber, then mix one of the six pieces of black Granitex to this mixture until well blended. Set aside.

5 Create the off-white egg: Mix 1" ball of ecru with 1" ball pearl white, then mix one of the six pieces of black Granitex to this mixture until well blended. Set aside.

6 Create the faux granite egg: Mix 1" ball of pearl white with 1" ball raw umber, then mix one piece of black Granitex to the mixure until well blended.

NOTE: For the faux granite egg, do not mix thoroughly. You want some of the variations of color to show through. When you have reached a stage where the color mix resembles "granite," quit mixing. Then mix one of the six pieces of black Granitex to this mixture until blended. Set aside.

Pearl white adds an inner luster to your eggs while the black Granitex adds a dull "egg-shell" texture and finish.

create the egg shapes

1. Place one newly made ball in the palm of your hands and roll until slightly warm to the touch. This should only take a few seconds.

2. Slowly move one end of your ball between your forefinger and thumb.

3. Roll gently to create the cone of the egg. Do not disturb the round shape of the rest of your ball. This will create an authentic egg shape.

4. Embellishments: Once the eggs have been baked, the pearl white/ecru egg can be coated with a thin layer of white acrylic craft paint. Natural eggs have an added dimension revealing the wealth that lies within. You can duplicate this effect by this simple technique. To add inclusions to your eggs, roll in pepper or instant coffee grounds. These inclusions add authenticity to your specimens.

5. Using a hatpin, pierce each end of the egg. Drill the hatpin through until the hole is open from end to end.

6. Using a skewer, re-drill the hole allowing each egg to rest on the skewer. You can place three newly formed eggs on each skewer.

7. Place your eggs on your toaster-oven baking pan.

make the secondary beads

1 Condition your clay.

2 Create one skewer of clay from ¼ package of each PREMO! color: ecru, pearl white, raw umber and black Granitex clay. *See Susan Ray's Basic Skewer Beads Instructions, page 137.*

3 Create seven beads 1" long x ¼" thick. Remove from skewer. Tap ends.

4 Place six beads onto the baking pan. Take the one remaining bead and roll in your palm to create a ball. Pierce with a skewer end to create hole.

5 Place remaining bead on toaster oven baking pan.

make three mini eggs for nest pendant

1 Condition clay.

2 Pick your three favorite egg color mixes and follow the same recipe used to make the full size eggs, this time adding together only a tiny pea-size ball of each color. Add some Granitex to each mixture.

3 Roll each ball into an egg shape. *(See Create the Egg Shapes on page 89.)*

4 To add dimension to eggs, roll them in pepper or instant coffee grounds. These inclusions add authenticity to your specimens.

make the nest pendant

1 Condition clay.

2 Mix the black and raw umber PREMO! until blended. Allow some of the color variations to remain.

3 Make the mixture into a ball. Reserve 1" x ¼" snake for assembling your pendant later.

4 Press the ball in the palm of your hand to flatten into a round disk.

5 Using the back of your thumb, create a well for the eggs to rest in.

6 Attach wire loop into pendant.

assemble the pendant

1 Carefully place the mini eggs side by side onto nest pendant.

2 Take the 1" x ¼" snake previously reserved and slightly flatten each end.

3 Create a loop by pressing the ends together. Attach the loop to the top of pendant by pressing in place. (For additional strength, a wire armature of 2" silver wire can be used.)

4 Place pendant onto the baking pan.

bake

1 Bake eggs, skewer beads, round bead and pendant following manufacturer's directions. Cool completely before removing from oven.

2 Use a large, fine emery board to smooth all sides of beads. Wipe clean.

necklace

supplies

6 large polymer eggs – various colors

1 tan 15 mm polymer round

6 tan 1" length x ½" diameter skewer beads

1 robin's egg nest with mini eggs, 1¼" diameter pendant

26 antique turquoise 5 mm x 3 mm ovals

21 turquoise foil-lined 13/0 seed beads

6 antique turquoise 2 mm heishe

26 silvertone 6 mm bicone spacers

1 silver toggle closure

30" of 7-strand .018 mm gauge flexible wire

2 sterling silver 3 mm ovals

4 sterling silver 2 mm x 3mm crimp beads

tool box

Flat nose pliers

Wire cutters

Crimping tool

Step-by-Step

See Basic Instructions, Single-Strand Necklace, page 146.

1 Attach one end of your toggle closure to the flexible wire using a crimp bead. Leave a 2" tail. Crimp in place. String one silver 2 mm x 3 mm oval and another crimp bead. String both short and long wires through the oval and a second crimp bead. Crimp the second crimp in place.

2 String one antique turquoise oval and cut away excess wire from short tail of flexible wire.

3 Continue to string beads as follows: One foil-lined turquoise 13/0 seed bead and one antique turquoise 5 mm x 3 mm oval.

4 Repeat above five times until you have seven antique turquoise ovals in place (including the oval which followed the second crimp bead).

5 Continue stringing: One silvertone 6 mm bicone spacer, one tan 1" length x ½" diameter skewer bead, one silvertone 6 mm bicone spacer and one antique turquoise 5 mm x 3 mm oval.

 For a shorter necklace, simply remove some of the ovals and seed beads. For a longer necklace, add more. This method will not disturb the design.

6 Repeat Step 5 three times, ending with an additional silvertone 6 mm bicone spacer.

7 String the eggs as follows: One polymer egg, one silvertone 6 mm bicone spacer and one antique turquoise 5 mm x 3 mm oval.

8 Repeat Step 7 two more times until three eggs are strung. End with one additional silvertone 6 mm bicone spacer.

9 String one 15 mm tan polymer round and one silvertone 6 mm bicone spacer.

10 Alternate heishe with foil-lined 13/0 seed beads five times.

11 Pass the wire through the robin's nest pendant and repeat Steps 1 through 10 in reverse to complete the other side of the necklace.

METAL/WIRE

chapter 4

"I am enough of an artist to draw freely upon my imagination. Imagination is more important than knowledge. Knowledge is limited. Imagination encircles the world." — Albert Einstein (1879 - 1955)

where have all the cowboys gone? bracelet

"One touch of nature makes the whole world kin." — *William Shakespeare*

Designer: Jessica Italia

Finished Size: 6¾", without clasp

Expense: Less than $50

Level of Expertise: Intermediate

Time to Complete: One day

KINSHIP

supplies

7 Bali silver 2 mm x 6 mm barrels

2 sterling silver 8 mm x 9 mm cowboy hats

2 sterling silver 6 mm stars

2 sterling silver 5 mm x 20 mm alligators

7 non-tarnish silver artistic 20-gauge wire, 2" sections

7 non-tarnish silver artistic 22-gauge wire, 2" sections

4 sterling silver 3 mm jump rings

2 sterling silver 2" head pins

1 sterling silver 5 mm soldered jump ring

tool box

Wire cutters

Chain nose pliers

Round nose pliers

Cimping tool

 tip

When creating "S"-hook links, use the tip of chain nose pliers to make a small loop. Use back end of round nose pliers to create the "S" form.

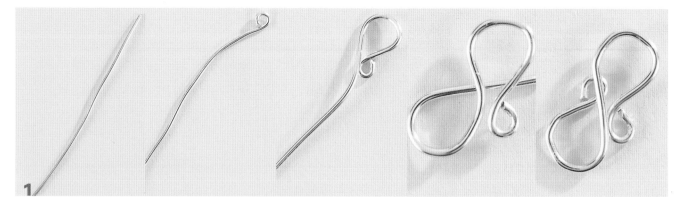

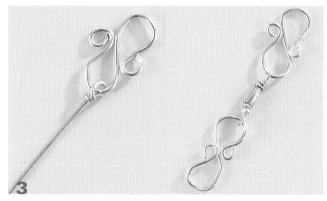

Step-by-Step

1 Using pliers and a 2" section of 20-gauge artistic wire, create a small loop on the end and bend wire around large end of pliers to make S-link. Create a second small loop on opposite end.

2 Repeat Step 1 six times (make one S-link larger than others for the clasp).

3 With the 2" sections of 22-gauge wire, string on barrels, center and loop around one end of S-link. Coil remaining wire around top of barrel.

4 Repeat Step 3 seven times. (One barrel will be looped and coiled to soldered jump ring and S-link. Large link should be on opposite end for clasp.)

5 Attach two stars to head pins and remaining charms to jump rings.

6 Attach charms with jump rings or head pins to S-links, start at clasp end (skip clasp, leave empty). Attach alligator, next link attach star with head pin, then cowboy hat, alligator, star and cowboy hat.

memory makers nature photo bracelet

MEMORABLE

"In order to make an apple pie from scratch, you must first create the universe."
— *Dr. Carl Sagan*

Designer: Susan Ray

Finished Size: 7½", without clasp

Expense: $25 - $100 (depends on the number of photo charms and whether sterling is used as the base metal)

Level of Expertise: Beginner

Time to Complete: One afternoon

supplies

1 sterling silver three-link clasp (Model is a slide version.)

4 sterling silver 2 mm x 3 mm crimp beads

14 silver 6 mm x 3 mm bicone spacers (includes two for dangles)

16 jet 8 mm faceted rounds

78 black 11/0 seed beads

2 sterling silver 3" head pins

24" of 7-strand .018 gauge flexible wire

tool box

Scissors

Paper clip

Access to color copier

Memory Maker kit

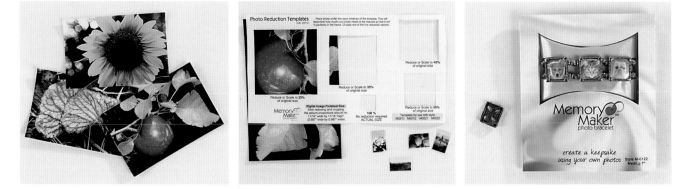

photo reduction system

1 Select a group of your favorite photos. Choose a subject that will fill most of the frame to make the best impression. Each Memory Maker kit comes with EZ-Fit Photo Reduction Template, designed to reduce your picture to the perfect size.

2 Choose reduction size. Place photo under the open windows of the template. Choose the area of the photo that you want to show in the frame. Of the five reduction options, pick the one you think will look best in the miniature frame.

3 Reduce photo on a color copier. Place photo and EZ Fit Photo Reduction Template face down in the color copier and set the reduction size to match the percentage listed under your selection. If necessary, secure photo to template with a small piece of tape to prevent picture from moving.

4 With scissors, trim reduced picture so no white border remains.

5 Place picture in frame. Remove protective acetate from the frame by using a straightened paper clip. Insert the paper clip through a hole in the back of the frame or side of the pendant and push forward to pop out acetate. Place picture in frame, making sure that the picture is securely positioned under corner taps. Replace acetate by inserting two corners first, then push slightly towards inserted corners so acetate will slightly bow. Remaining two corners should easily snap into place.

bracelet

Step-by-Step

1 Cut elastic away from Memory Maker's bracelet. Remove beads and photo charms.

2 *See Single-Strand Bracelet Instructions, page 146.* Secure crimp bead, string on all beads and spacers (see photo) and secure second crimp bead to other end.

3 Repeat the same technique for the second strand. (Even though this is a two-strand bracelet, it is strung as two single strands.)

4 Create two dangles. *(See Dangle Instructions, page 154)*

5 Insert dangles through each middle loop of the three-loop clasp. Be sure the dangles are short enough or they will interfere with the closure. Voila! A stunning photo charm bracelet for your favorite prints.

celestial
bodies choker

INTRIGUING

"In a pond koi can reach lengths of eighteen inches. Amazingly, when placed in a lake, koi can grow to three feet long. The metaphor is obvious. You are limited by how you see the world." — Vince Poscente

Designer: Barbara Markoe

Finished Size: 17", without clasp

Expense: More than $50

Level of Expertise: Intermediate

Time to Complete: 2 hours

supplies

6 lampwork 10 mm to 15 mm beads

4 sterling silver balls

2 Bali silver 6 mm x 8 mm beads

2 silver 6 mm x 8 mm beads

2 green 8 mm ceramic beads

2 teal 12 mm ceramic spacer discs

2 teal 8 mm ceramic spacer discs

18 Bali silver 6 mm to 12 mm spacer beads, various

19" of 14-gauge sterling silver round wire, dead soft (for base wire)

9" sterling silver coiled 24-gauge round wire, dead soft (see helpful tips below)

4 sterling silver ½" pieces coiled 20-gauge round wire, dead soft (see helpful tips below)

2 sterling silver ½" pieces twisted 22-gauge wire, dead soft (see helpful tips below)

NOTE: Make sure that all beads fit onto 14-gauge wire.

for charms

1 green 12 mm x 12 mm faceted chalcedony

3 sapphire 4 mm Indian bicone crystals

1 sterling silver Hilltribe charm

3 sterling silver 24-gauge 2" head pins

6 Bali silver 3 mm to 8 mm spacers

1 Norwegian Bokmal sterling silver 8 mm soldered ring

1 sterling silver 8 mm jump ring

tool box

Round nose pliers

Chain nose pliers

Wire cutters

Flush cutters

File (or a fine emery board)

Chasing hammer

Steel bench block

to create your bracelet

The Coiling Gizmo *(See Resources, page 160.)*

Econo Winder manual

safety

The tools described here seem harmless; however, it is highly recommended that you wear safety glasses when using them. Tools can break and send metal flying.

understanding terms

Wire and metals that come in sheets are measured with the term "gauge." The higher the number, the thinner the metal. For example, a 6-gauge wire is .162 of an inch thick and a 20-gauge wire is .032 of an inch thick.

Step-by-Step

a note about flush cutters

Cut a wire as shown. The wire on the right has a diamond shape.

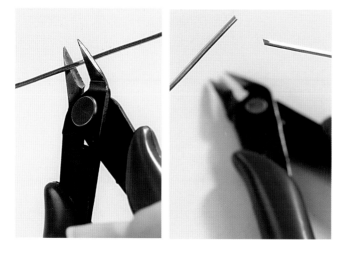

wire suggestions

Begin with copper wire and get a feel for it before moving to precious metals. You can use an assortment of gauges. With sterling, try starting with 20-gauge wrapping wire. You can use the same 20-gauge wire for the core or 16- or 18-gauge wire.

set up the
econo winder

make your first bead

1 Use a 20-gauge or thinner wire. Since wire comes in coils, you need to keep your coil from getting tangled. Wear the wire like a bracelet or put it on the floor, but put it around something like a quart jar. I use a metal thermos.

2 Take the end of the wire and push it through the eye of the cranking rod. Then wrap the end of the wire around the eye.

3 Insert the thin crank into the two smallest holes of the bracket frame and begin to crank. Notice how the left thumb is placed over the wire and against the bracket. As you crank, the wire will automatically feed itself and produce a coil spring.

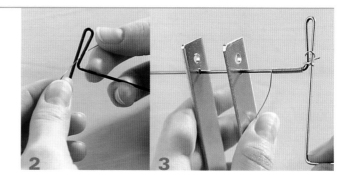

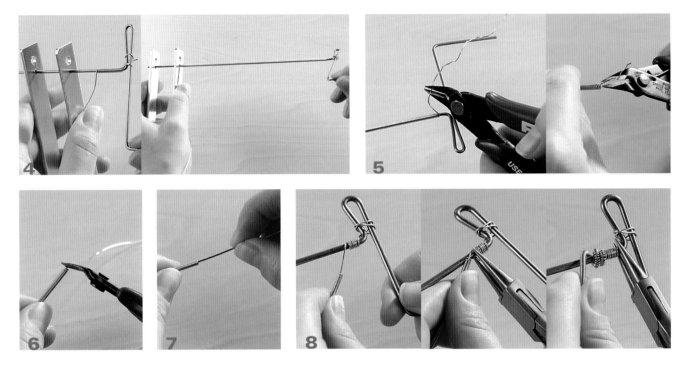

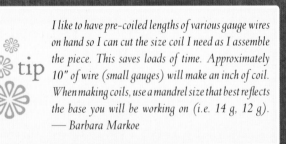

4 Continue cranking. The length of the coil spring is 5". (You can make shorter coiled lengths for smaller beads.)

5 Snip the wire on the right side of the crank at the beginning of the coil, then pull the coil spring off. Look at the end of the spring that you just snipped. You need to do one more snip to make it look good. Insert the tip of the cutters into the spring. You want to snip just one wire. Remember to have the flush side toward the coils.

6 Warning: You don't want little pieces of metal to fly off when you cut, so cover the whole thing with your hand before snipping the wire. Now go to the left end of the coil and snip the long wire from that end.

7 Slip a core wire into the coil spring. It can be the same gauge as you were using or thicker. For a bead with a 5" coil spring, a core wire of 20 gauge or thicker is recommended. (Thinner core wires make beads of this size too soft.) The core wire can remain uncut.

tip

I like to have pre-coiled lengths of various gauge wires on hand so I can cut the size coil I need as I assemble the piece. This saves loads of time. Approximately 10" of wire (small gauges) will make an inch of coil. When making coils, use a mandrel size that best reflects the base you will be working on (i.e. 14 g, 12 g).
— Barbara Markoe

8 Take the thicker cranking rod and thread the core wire into the eye as you did previously. Begin to crank, holding the crankshaft in your left hand and coiling the core wire a few times. To create a tight coil on the end of your bead, take your chain nose pliers and grip the crank. Push the wire toward the pliers with your left hand.

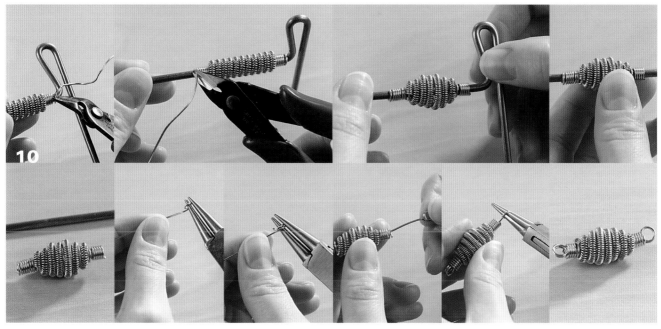

creating a double coil

9 To start the double coil, twist the previously coiled section of wire around the crank with your left hand. Then grab that coil with the thumb and forefinger of your right hand.

10 Turn the rod with your thumb and forefinger and coil to the end. You can now grab the crank and make some additional coils on the left side of the bead with the core wire. Match the number of coils on the left end with the number on the right.

11 Snip the wire on the right. Go into the coil and snip as you did in Step 5. Remove the long wire on the other end. Now you have a double-coil cylinder bead.

Step-by-Step

1 When adding beads to bangles, just "go with the flow," although you may choose to lay out your bead design. Each side should measure about 5½" for this project.

2 Start with the 19" piece of 14-gauge wire. Flatten one end of the wire with chasing hammer and steel bench block. With the tip of the chain nose pliers, create a loop at the end where the wire is flat. In the back or largest part of round nose pliers, form a loop in the opposite direction from the small loop made previously. You now have a hook for your bangle. With chain nose pliers, add one or two small bends after the hook. This will help serve as a bead stop.

3 Clip about an inch from the 9-foot 24-gauge wrapped wire. Slip it onto the base mandrel, all the way over small bends up to the hook. The wrap should fit snugly over the bends.

4 Start adding your beads and ½" coils onto the base mandrel. After the first-half of the beads are added, clip 6" from the 24-gauge coil. Add the coil onto base mandrel. Add remaining set of beads. You should be left with about 1½" to 2" of mandrel that will form the end loop. If you have NOT pre-designed, then check your balance. Make any spacing adjustments.

5 Flatten remaining end of the wire with chasing hammer and steel bench block. Add the remaining 2" of 24-gauge coil. Clip excess coil so the flattened end sticks out about ¼". With the tip of the chain nose pliers, create a loop at the end where the wire is flat. This should now be holding everything in place. With a large mandrel, finger or wooden dowel, form a large loop in the opposite direction from the small loop previously made. This is the trickiest part!

6 Adjust hook and loop so it sits properly on the neck.

7 Adding charms: Using the head pins, string a variety of charms. Wire-wrap them onto the soldered jump ring. Connect this dangle to the large loop with another jump ring.

confetti earrings

GENIUS

"When Nature has work to be done, she creates a genius to do it."
— *Ralph Waldo Emerson*

Designer: Barbara Markoe

Finished Size: 1¼"

Expense: Less than $50

Level of Expertise: Intermediate

Time to Complete: 1-2 hours

supplies

4 ivory 4 mm to 6 mm freshwater pearls

4 pink 4 mm to 6 mm freshwater pearls

4 light pink AB 4 mm bicone crystals

4 clear AB 4 mm bicone crystals

10 to 12 various Bali silver 2 mm to 6 mm nuggets or rounds

50 seed beads in a color variety within the palette

20-gauge sterling silver round wire, dead soft (4 or 5 times your finished length)

24-gauge sterling silver round wire, dead soft (4 or 5 times your finished length)

2 sterling silver ear wires

tool box

Round nose pliers

Chain nose pliers

Flat nose pliers

Wire cutters

Ruler

Step-by-Step

1 Start with a 4½" length of 20-gauge wire. This will form the base of your earring. On one end form a small loop using round nose pliers (the smaller the better). With the flat pliers, bend the loop a slight angle to the wire.

2 Loop remaining length through newly created "eye," leaving about 1½" sticking out the top. This is the length that will attach to the ear wire. Decide what shape you want, i.e., round or teardrop, etc. Adjust and shape (you will need to re-adjust at the end).

3 With the 1½" piece, make a small loop with round nose pliers. Insert ear wire into loop and wire wrap down to "eye" to secure. You should have a plain "hoop" earring. Repeat for earring two.

4 Take about 15" of 24-gauge wire. Start by wrapping the wire three or four times at one end of the hoop. As you continue, start to add beads randomly: A few seeds, a bicone, a pearl, wrapping between each section. It may take a few wraps to get the hang of it. Remember, "organic" is the word. If you run out of wire, simply start another piece in the same manner. These earrings are wrapped two times (forward and back). Clean up ends with wire cutters. Re-adjust shape if necessary.

noe lani bracelet

COASTAL

"Forests, lakes, and rivers, clouds and winds, stars and flowers, stupendous glaciers and crystal snowflakes - every form of animate or inanimate existence, leaves its impress upon the soul of man."
— Orison Sweet Marden

Designer: Barbara Markoe

Lampwork Artist: Karen Leonardo

Finished Size:, 7½", without clasp

Expense: $50 or more

Level of Expertise: Intermediate

Time to Complete: 1-2 hours

Color Palette: All silver except for the fantastic focal that ranges from pale green to deep blue.

supplies

1 focal 30 mm x 22 mm lampwork bead

40 sterling silver 2 mm to 4 mm balls

2 Bali silver 10 mm disk or ball beads for ends

10" of 12-gauge sterling silver round wire, dead soft (for base or mandrel wire; see helpful tips)

36" of 20-gauge sterling silver round wire, dead soft

36" of 24-gauge sterling silver round wire, dead soft

4" of 14-gauge sterling silver round wire, dead soft

Note: Bead holes must be large enough to accommodate 12-gauge wire.

tool box

Round nose pliers

Chain nose pliers

Coiling Gizmo *(See Coiling Gizmo Instructions, page 101.)*

Wire cutters

File (or fine emery board)

Chasing hammer

Steel bench block

The length of your mandrel or base wire will depend on the size of your wrist, the size of the beads you use and how loose you like your bangle to hang. There is no easy way to calculate this, so if you've never made a bangle, you should make a sample using copper wire.

Step-by-Step

make the base

1 Take 10" piece of 12-gauge wire and flush cut both ends. A 10" piece of mandrel will fit about a 7" wrist when complete with small (10 mm to 11 mm) beads or a 6½" wrist with large beads. With the large end of the round nose pliers, make a loop or eye on one end of the mandrel. Make another loop at the other end, after you have added the beads.

2 Figure out how much space you need to cover. Measure the mandrel from loop joint to where the end loop joint will be. Example: The measurement is 8". Measure the length of your focal bead. My focal was about 1¼" long. Now subtract that measurement from your mandrel length of 8". That leaves 6¾" of mandrel to cover with wire. Divide that by 2 (either side of the focal). That leaves approx 3⅞" of space on each side of the focal. You will need this measurement to do your initial coiling of the mandrel and then simply assemble it. Remember, you need to consider adjusting this measurement if you are adding large beads or spacers at the ends.

3 Divide the 36" of 20-gauge wire into two equal 18" pieces. With the Coiling Gizmo and a mandrel the size of your 12-gauge wire or larger, start wrapping one piece of wire, wrapping evenly three or four times to get started. Then continue in an uneven, haphazard way to the magic length of 3⅞" (remember that measurement). You should be about half way into your piece of wire. Now wrap back in the same manner, overlapping the first wrap. When you get to the end of the wire, find an inconspicuous spot to tuck it in. Use pliers to reach in and give it an extra squeeze. Remove from Gizmo and angle-cut end. Repeat with other piece of 20-gauge wire. You now have two pieces of coiled wire about 3⅞" long.

assembly

1. Holding the loop end of the mandrel, add one Bali or spacer bead. Add one of the new coils, with the "even end" first, next to the spacer. Add focal bead, second coil, with the "even" side toward the end, and end spacer. You should have enough wire to make a loop and secure the pieces.

2 It now looks close to a finished piece. Divide 24-gauge wire into two equal pieces. With one piece, start about a third of the way up the base coil on one side, weaving and coiling, adding little silver balls as you go. You may choose to overlap your focal as I did. When you come to the end of the wire, simply find a place to tuck and secure. Again, use pliers to give it an extra squeeze. Do the same for the other side.

6

make the clasp

1 Flatten one end of the wire with chasing hammer and steel bench block.

2 With the tip of the chain nose pliers, create a loop at the end where the wire is flat.

3 In the back or largest part of the round nose pliers, form a loop in the opposite direction from the small loop made previously.

4 Grasp the other end of the wire with the tip of the round or chain nose pliers. Have as little of the wire peeking through the end of the pliers as possible. Now, begin coiling the wire. Grasping your developing coil with your chain nose pliers, continue to coil until you measure 1⅝" from end to end.

5 Grasp the wire next to coil with chain nose pliers. With your left thumb pressing against the tail of the wire, form a bend. Grasp the loop with large round nose pliers and gently urge the wire to rest next to the coil. Partially close the clasp with the round nose pliers.

6 Use chasing hammer to flatten the curve of loop and also the bend at the bottom of the clasp. Open one eye on bangle and insert clasp through the bottom "V" section. Close the eye.

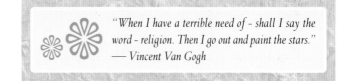

northern lights earrings

SPIRITUAL

"The Sun, with all those planets revolving around it, and dependent on it, can still ripen a bunch of grapes as though it had nothing else in the Universe to do."
— Galileo Galilei

Designer: Roberta Ogborn

Finished Size: 1⅛" x ¾"

Expense: More than $50

Level of Expertise: Beginner/Intermediate

Time to Complete: One weekend

supplies

1 piece ½" x 3" Dichroic glass

2 white 4 mm cubic zirconias

1 pkg. (16 grams) PMC3

1 PMC3 syringe type clay

8 pieces pure (.999) silver casting grains

1 pair sterling silver ear wires

tool box

1 glazed ceramic 4" x 4" tile

1 small bowl of water

1 jeweler's file

1 X-acto knife with new blade

1 240 to 600 grit sanding block

1 burnisher, for polishing finished project

1 small liner paintbrush

1 pair of tweezers

1 PMC Crafter's Station and Torch

Several cotton swabs

1 respirator mask, for use in sanding

1 glass cutter

1 hand-held hair dryer

1 silver-polishing cloth

1 brass-cleaning brush (found in most auto parts stores)

tip

All but one of the tools listed are optional...in other words you may substitute any object that will accomplish the same purpose as the tool stated, i.e.: Sanding block = sandpaper, X-acto = straight bladed knife, etc. If you already have a ceramic kiln, or any other firing device that is capable of reaching and sustaining 1290 degrees of heat, it may be used. There also are usually a number of ceramicists in your area that fire for a price. Use a respirator: Sanding clay or glass causes particles too tiny to see with the naked eye to float in the air around you. You do not want these in your lungs.

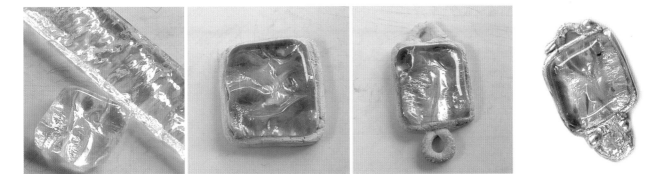

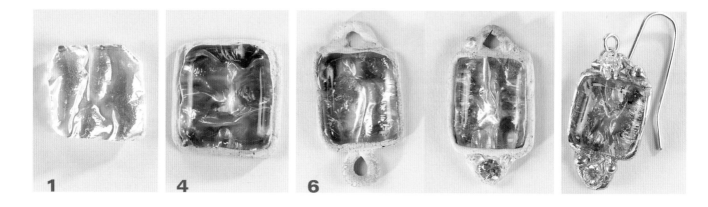

1   4   6

dichroic glass

Most towns have a stained glass supply house in their area and they usually carry dichroic. It is sold by the inch and a 1" x 3" piece of glass is very economical. Look for bags of "scrap" that will provide many projects. If you are not familiar with cutting glass, ask them to cut it for you. You will need two ½" square pieces to complete this project. Ebay and any number of Web sites also have dichro. Got a favorite glass heirloom that you've been meaning to glue back together? Make it last forever by using it in a piece of PMC jewelry. Dichroic MUST be pre-fired to preserve the iridescent coating. If you cannot pre-fire any other kind of glass, you must sand the sharpness off the edges and corners. Most any sandpaper or sanding block will do, but wet-dry emery cloth is the best and quickest. These pieces will be fired with the clay in place, and if they are sharp before the firing process, they will be even sharper after being fired.

Step-by-Step

prepare the clay base

1 Open package of PMC3 clay and break off a pea-sized piece (about the size of an 8 mm to 10 mm bead) Rewrap the rest of the clay to keep it from drying out.

2 Lay the "pea" on the 4" square tile and roll it under your finger until you have a "worm" of clay, approximately 2" long and ⅛" thick.

3 Wrap this clay around the edges of one piece of your prepared glass.

4 Overlap the ends of the worm, and using the X-acto or a sharp knife, cut the clay at a slight angle where it overlaps itself. Use a liner brush dipped in water to moisten the ends of the clay and then smooth the clay, either with a knife or the brush so the join is completely sealed. Use the flat blade of the knife (sharp edge facing down on the tile) to push the clay up against the glass all the way around. The clay will shrink some, so you do not want this "bezel" to be too tight, but you don't want obvious gaps either.

5 Take the balance of your clay worm and make a "V" shape and an "O" shape. The "V" will be turned upside down and its legs will be joined to the top of the piece with little dabs of paste from the syringe, while the "O" shape will be joined to the bottom of the piece in the same manner. The "O" is where you will mount your 4 mm CZ, so you want it small enough to encircle the CZ and leave the back of the stone open, but not so big that the stone falls through when you set it.

6 Use a hair dryer to dry the piece. Aim and shoot the hot air over the piece until it is dry. When dry, use the blade of a knife (flat against the surface of the tile) to gently loosen the piece from the tile. If any pieces break off, use a dab of paste from the syringe to "glue" it back on.

sanding

1 PLEASE wear a respirator at this point. When it is off of the tile and completely dry, sand the back and smooth out any unevenness in the clay. Remove little marks made by tools, fingernails, etc., that you don't want in your finished project. Be sure to clean every scrap of silver off the back of the glass. The silver will bond with the glass, so you don't want any stray spots on the front or back of the glass to mess up your design.

2 When the piece is smoothed to your satisfaction, use the liner brush dipped in a little water to give the back a completely smooth finish. If you desire a highly polished look in your finished project, dry with hairdryer.

set the stone

1 Set the piece on the tile, front side up. Use a liner brush dipped in water to moisten the "O" on the bottom of the piece. Use the paste in the syringe to lay a small line of paste around the circumference of the "O." Immediately, pick up a CZ with a pair of tweezers and gently lay it into the paste. Take the tip of the knife or the end of the paintbrush, if it is small enough, and gently push the stone into the paste clay until the clay pushes up and over the girdle of the stone. This is known as a "bezel" set stone. If it is done right, when the clay fires and does its shrinkage trick, it is the most secure way to set the stone.

2 Dry the piece with the hairdryer and smooth with sandpaper or block. (Again, wearing the respirator.) Once smooth, put a dab of syringe paste on each leg of the upside down "V" and push a piece of casting grain into each dab of paste. Do the same on either side of the "O" on the bottom. At this point, use the knife or the end of a paintbrush to gently "settle" the casting grains into the paste, using a bit of a rocking motion to push out any air that might be trapped underneath the grain. This makes a better contact and more secure setting of the silver grains.

3 Use a liner brush dipped in water to gently smooth any paste that might be sticking out around the embellishments. Dry with hairdryer. Be sure to inspect the piece carefully. Smooth any sharp edges and clean both surfaces of the glass as well as the front and back of the stone. Not all of the stone has to be open in the back, but the more open it is, the more light refraction, sparkle and dazzle!

fire the jewelry

1 Fire the piece according to the directions in the PMC3 package. The instruction sheet will describe several different ways of firing the jewelry. When completely cool, use the brass-cleaning brush to remove the "fire scale" and you will see the shiny silver color develop right before your eyes! Leave as is (a sort of "satin" finish) or burnish it with a burnisher or any piece of smooth stainless steel to a high-gloss silver shine. Polish with a silver-polishing cloth and attach to a sterling silver earring finding.

pennsylvania fiddleheads brooch

SUBLIME

"Nature always wears the colors of the spirit." — *Ralph Waldo Emerson*

Designer: Lynn Larkins

Finished Size: 2⅞" x 2"

Expense: Less than $50

Level of Expertise: Beginner/Intermediate

Time to Complete: Weekend

supplies

25 grams Slow Dry Art Clay Silver

5 to 6 grams Paste Type Silver

3 to 4 grams Syringe Silver

5 fireable 5 mm peridots

35 mm brooch finding

1 teaspoon peacock green Thompson enamel

1 teaspoon lime yellow Thompson enamel

1 teaspoon Vandyke brown Thompson enamel

tool box

Paintbrushes: 1 small round, 1 flat

Acrylic roller

X-acto knife or sharp knife

Clay spatula or pick

Teflon sheets

Badger balm or olive oil

Plastic wrap

Tweezers

Rubber block

Kiln

Ammonia

Hair dryer

Small sifter

Heat glove

Hair dryer

Small sifter

Long firing fork

Klyr-Fire

Pick and tongs

Fiber blanket

Pencil and paper

Glass-scratch brush or old toothbrush

tip

Slow Dry dries five times slower than regular clay, so you have more time to work with it before it starts to dry. If you're in hot, dry areas, and regular clay dries in 5 minutes, you have about 20-25 minutes, or if it's humid where you live, you have lots more time. Keep in mind too, that it will take longer under the hair dryer or in the food dehydrator and you must be sure it is ABSOLUTELY dry before you fire it.

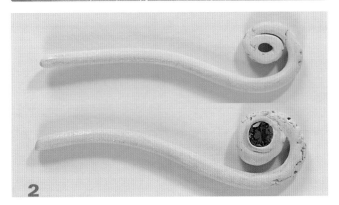

2

Step-by-Step

1 Set up your workspace with a large Teflon sheet on a hard staple surface. Fill a small glass jar with 1" of water to store open syringe, wet brushes and silver filings. Make a chenille stem model or use photo for a guide. Have several small Teflon sheets ready as you finish each frond for drying. Rub a small amount of Badger balm on fingers and on the acrylic roller for rolling the worms.

2 Cut off 3½ grams of Slow Dry. Wrap the rest tightly in plastic wrap. Knead the clay to warm and form in a small roll. Place on the large Teflon sheet and roll it into a long worm with the acrylic roller. When it's 3¼" long, transfer to a small sheet and shape with the coil curving to the left. The Slow Dry tends to spring back, but with a little coaxing it will stay. With the tweezers, "pinch" texture into the clay coil top and sides, being careful not to go all the way through. At this point the frond will be drying. If you have finger or nail marks on the clay, take a little watered down paste and smooth with the flat brush. If using peridots, determine where they will go on the coil, making sure there's a hole through them so light can pass. With the syringe, make a circle around the opening. Using tweezers, drop the stone into the hole. Make sure the girdle (widest part of the stone) is covered. If not, make another pass around with the syringe. Put the syringe back into the water jar. Place in dryer.

3 Repeat Step 1 with 3½ g of clay, but 4" long, coil to the left. At this point, be sure to think about how the stems will touch.

4 Repeat Step 1 with 5 g of clay, 5" long. Coil to the right with an open hook. If the first two pieces are dry enough to pick up, put them next to this frond and make sure several points are touching. If not, adjust the third piece to fit the first two pieces.

5 Repeat Step 1 with 5 g of clay, 4" long, so it will be thicker, coiled left.

6 Repeat Step 1 with 7 g of clay, 4½" long, thickest, and open coil to right.

7 When all are dry, fill cracks or dings with paste. Smooth out, leaving the texture on the coils and anywhere else. Dry. Begin sanding. Start with 400, working up to 1200. This is very important at this stage, as once pasted together it will be difficult to sand. The more finishing done now, the better the finished piece will be. What goes into the kiln, comes out of the kiln, it does not "smooth" in the heat. Be sure the texture on the coil is smooth so it doesn't snag on clothes.

8 Place four of the sanded fronds on a piece of paper with the stems touching, put the fifth piece on top. When you like what you see, draw around the fronds with a pencil, noting where you have to paste. Put two pieces on a Teflon sheet. Put paste on both parts that touch and slide together. Dry.

9 Do this for all four fronds, drying completely. Carefully turn the piece over and put on the Teflon. Wherever you have a joint, fill in with paste for more strength, keeping in mind you don't want to see this on the front. Dry. Repeat, until you have a strong, smooth bridge where pieces touch. When dry and secure, sand smooth, inspecting the front and sides, keeping fronds round. Add fifth frond to the top and paste as before, being careful not to have extra paste showing. You will have to do several thin pastings here to control the smoothness on the front. When this is dry, turn over and see if there are places to add paste, securing the fifth frond to the main piece so it doesn't show on the front. Dry and sand as before.

10 At this point you should have a fairly well-done piece, but this is where the needle files really come in handy. They can get into all the little crevices and make them smooth. Be careful handling the coils, as they are delicate. If you press too hard, they may break — one did on me! Just paste them back together and re-sand. It may take more than one paste and dry sequence, but be patient, it works just fine.

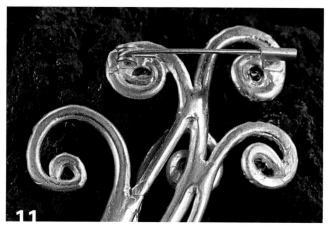

11 If satisfied with the appearance, turn over and plan the placement of the brooch finding. You'll need an area for a little "pad" where each side will sit. Don't cover a stone. Check alignment with the "pin" part and place the side with the two bumps between the tap in a blob of paste, making sure the paste comes up through the little holes in the bottom. Let dry, and re-paste, making sure the base is covered. Sand smooth. Put the "pin" part into the space, tail up. Line up the hood side and mark with a little bit of paste. Remove the "pin" and paste the hood part as the other side. DO NOT ATTACH the "pin" part now — it cannot be fired. Set aside. Dry all pasted parts and sand smooth.

12 Place the dry, smooth piece, stone side up, on the fiber blanket, leveling it with small bits of fiber paper to compensate for the brooch finding. Make sure there are no fronds hanging out unsupported. Don't force anything; just be sure everything is supported on the blanket. Fire from room temperature, full to 1600 degrees for 10 minutes, or 1560 degrees for 20 minutes. Take it out as soon as it's done. Let cool.

13 If you are going to enamel the pin, get things set up while the pin is in the kiln, and/or cooling. I didn't want to cover the whole piece, only suggest color in the coils. You can apply more, if desired. Have your three colors cleaned, following regular enameling directions.

14 Finish the cooled silver: Using a rubber block, brush the firing residue from the whole piece. Don't leave any white. Tumble it for 1¾ hours, or you can burnish it and use the power tools. If you choose NOT to enamel, then put the "pin" in place. Insert with the tail down. Press the two sides together with pliers — snug, but not too tight.

15 Enameling: Thompson recommends heat between 1400 and 1500 degrees, since each kiln will vary. Remember, each time the door opens, the temperature drops.

16 Clean your silver before enameling. Wash with a mix of ammonia and water with a glass scratch brush or old toothbrush to remove any oil or dirt. Rinse with clean water and dry COMPLETELY (hair dryer will do). Make sure there are no water drops in the crevices.

17 Place the pin on a piece of white paper so you can save your excess. I apply a thin coat of Klyr-Fire on the area I want to coat (the first firing only) it helps the powder stick. Be careful not to put it on the peridots. Put a little peacock green enamel in the small sifter, run a pick over the twisted handle. When the silver is covered with a thin coat, stop. With a clean, dry brush, make sure there is no powder on the stones or on the silver where you don't want it. It may not show now, but it will after it's fired! Put the pin in the trivet on top of the firing rack and put on top of the kiln to dry.

18 When dry, using heat glove and long firing fork, open the door and place the rack in the kiln. Again, with glove and long fork, remove from kiln and check if powder looks granular, if so, put back in for 60 more seconds. Mark down the time. When fired to smooth, remove to a safe surface. Using tongs, take the pin off the trivet, as it will cool faster. Remember, it is VERY HOT.

19 When completely cooled, repeat above step (without Klyr-Fire) using lime yellow enamel. Fire and cool.

20 The third firing: Put on a light coat of Vandyke brown enamel, especially in the coil recesses, to mute the two greens. Fire the same way again. Cool.

21 At this point, if you're happy, stop. If not, add more enamel where you want it. You'll notice the silver has a slight matte look to it, it's not white like after a full firing, but it has lost the shine and may even be slightly rough. Use the power tool to burnish. The shine comes right back. If it's still a little rough, you probably have some enamel dust on it. It may come off with some filing — no guarantees. Now put "pin" in place following the directions in Step 14.

GLASS

chapter 5

"Heaven is under our feet as well as over our heads."
— *Henry David Thoreau*

water and beach pebbles bracelet

VERSATILE

"Nature teaches more than she preaches. There are no sermons in stones. It is easier to get a spark out of a stone than a moral." — *John Burroughs*

Designer: Tamara Knight

Lampwork Artist: Tamara Knight

Finished Size: 9", without the clasp*

Expense: $50 to $100

Level of Expertise: Intermediate

Time to Complete: Three hours in studio, plus a walk on the beach

*Due to the girth of the stones, this bracelet must be sized bigger than usual. It will fit a 7½" to 8" wrist.

supplies

2 sterling-silver 6 mm x 9 mm totem beads

20 sterling silver 3 mm x 1 mm saucer beads

10 blue-toned Boro beads, a mixture of sizes: 6 mm to 12 mm

20 beach pebbles with hole size ranges, not more than 4 mm thick x 12 mm wide

12" piece of flexible 49-strand .024 40 lb. wire

2 sterling silver 2 mm x 2 mm crimp beads

1 sterling silver 15 mm toggle clasp

tool box

3/32 diamond bit

Dremel tool

Basin of water

Eye protection

Crimping pliers

tip Often lampwork beads have large holes. If your lampwork beads lay on the strand sloppily, fashion seed beads can be used inside the holes to help center the beads. Usually 8/0 seed beads work well.

Step-by-Step

See Basic Stringing Instructions, Single-Strand Bracelet, page 146.

1 If your pebbles are soft enough, a ³⁄₃₂ pointed diamond bit can be used on a Dremel tool to drill holes. Follow manufacturer's directions. I prefer the holes to not be in the center. Wear eye protection and drill under water. You may wish to consult a lapidary supply store about the stone hardness in your area.

2 Attach one end of the flexible wire to the toggle clasp. One of the sterling totem beads will go between the crimp and the toggle. The order is: crimp bead, totem bead, toggle clasp, back through the totem bead, then back through the crimp bead and crimp. This will allow more length between beads and the toggle for ease in use. The extra bead also protects your crimp bead from wearing down the flexible wire.

3 In random ones, twos and threes, lay out the stones with a Boro water bead between. One saucer bead goes on each side of the Boro bead. String as follows: two stones, saucer, Boro bead, saucer bead, three stones, saucer bead, Boro bead, saucer bead, stones. The saucer bead will protect the Boro beads from being worn down against the stone and add a little sparkle.

4 After stacking the balance of the beads, add the toggle clasp, crimp and totem bead. The order is: crimp bead, totem bead and toggle clasp, back through the totem bead, then back through the crimp bead. Due to the depth of the beads, there are two things to consider before you crimp. First, the overall length of the bracelet should be about an inch longer then you would normally wear due to the depth of the beads. Second, due to the depth of the beads, the strand should be snug, not tight. If the beads are too tight, you will not be able to flex the bracelet while wearing it around your wrist — the wire will stress and break. To prevent this problem, put the bracelet on your wrist and flex it before crimping.

NOTE: *For other examples of Tamara Knight's lampwork, please see the* "The Art and Soul of Glass Beads" *(KP Books).*

petals necklace and bracelet set

CONTEMPORARY

"Every flower is a soul blossoming in nature." —Gerard De Nerval

Designer: Ilene Baranowitz

Finished Size: Necklace: 18" long; Bracelet: 7" to 8" (stretch)

Expense: Less than $50

Level of Expertise: Beginner/ Intermediate

Time to Complete: One weekend

supplies

Faux Dichro Liquid Glass Luminous Elements, Faux Dichro Hi Gloss or Pro's Choice Topcoat

Parchment paper or other non-stick surface

Laminated black lip shell graduated fan (set of 7 pieces for necklace)

Laminated black lip shell components (set of 9 pieces for bracelet)

.012 mm flexible wire for wisps

.019 mm flexible wire for beading

12 gold 4 to 5 mm bead caps for the necklace

.5 mm elastic Powercord

60 light pink 6/0 seed beads, for bracelet

80 Dyna Mites translucent rainbow cream soda 11/0 seed beads

50 Delica rainbow white silky satin beads

40 gold 4 mm beads

40 (Beadery brand) 6 mm to 8 mm mixed metallic beads

G-S Hypo-Tube Cement or Beacon Glass, Metal and More or 2-part epoxy

8 crimp beads for necklace

Toggle clasp for necklace

tool box

Adhesive tape

Sharp scissors, such as Kai scissors

Tweezers

Crimping pliers

Beading pliers

Wire cutters, preferably side cutters

Ruler

The .012 mm cord is very soft and flexible. The points are rounded and will not cause any discomfort when wearing either the necklace or the bracelet.

preparation

Apply Faux Dichro to the surface of all black lip shell pieces following manufacturer's directions. Faux Dichro glass jewels require no heat, no kiln and less expense. Four easy steps to completion: 1) Apply Liquid Glass to your surface; 2) Place layers of Luminous Elements onto Liquid Glass; 3) Apply more Liquid Glass; 4) Apply Hi Gloss Finish Coat. *See Resources on page 160, Creative Spirit Crafts, for more information about Faux Dichro glass jewels.*

necklace

Step-by-Step

1 Cut a 20" piece of the .019 mm flexible wire. Tie off one end temporarily with a knot to secure strung beads. Lay out the fan pieces so they are in the correct graduating order with the longest pieces in the center and shorter pieces on each side. Starting with the fan pieces, string one short fan piece, two bead caps with large end next to fan pieces and short sides facing each other, or use one barbell bead. String the next fan piece. Repeat with all fan pieces, divided by the bead caps or barbells, until all fan pieces are strung.

2 String one gold bead alternating with one metallic bead for a total length of 7½". Slide all beads to the end of the side, leaving approximately 1" of wire. Add one crimp bead and attach one side of the clasp to the end.

3 Open the knot on the other side of the necklace and add 7½" to this side, as before, with a crimp bead and other half of the clasp.

4 Cut two pieces of .012 flexible wire, each 2" long. Fold one piece in half and wrap around the necklace between the first fan section and the gold bead adjacent to it. Thread one crimp bead over both ends; pull tight to the top of the wrap and crimp. Repeat with the other 2" section on the other side of the fan.

5 Cut 12 pieces of the .012 cord. Holding two cords together, wrap around the center of the space between the two bead caps adjacent to the next two fan pieces. Add one crimp bead, bring to the top, and crimp tightly. Repeat for the rest of the fan.

6 Trim each strand at random lengths between each fan piece and the two sides. Separate the strands by hand. This will give the wisps a feathered look instead of all lengths being uniform.

7 With the pinpoint of the Hypo-Tube Cement, or a toothpick dipped in either Beacon Glass, Metal and More or 2-part epoxy, put a small amount of glue in the center of each of the four tails. Thread a small seed bead or Delica bead on each piece until it reaches the glue dab in the center of the strand. Put a dab on the tip of each strand followed by another bead, randomly selecting the Delica or rainbow cream soda size 11/0 bead. Use two beads on the longer strand and one bead on the shorter strand on the ends of both strands. There should now be four strands and eight beads between each fan piece and two strands and three beads on each end of the fan. Allow to dry thoroughly. "Fluff" to separate, carefully separating and slightly bending the strands.

bracelet

Step-by-Step

1 Cut a piece of elastic cord approximately 6" long. Tie a knot in one end. Begin by stringing one 6/0 bead followed by one 11/0 bead; repeat until there are four 6/0 beads and three 11/0 beads ending with a 6/0 bead. Run the elastic thread through bottom hole on the side of the first bracelet component and repeat the beading, same as on the strand. You will have four 6/0 beads alternating with three 11/0 beads on this side of the component. Run the elastic through the top of the component and tie tightly to the knot at the beginning of the strand. Apply a dab of glue next to where the knot meets the component and push knot inside the hole to hide. Cut the cord. Set component aside.

2 With another 6" piece of elastic, thread the same way you began previously, with four 6/0 beads and three 11/0 beads. Thread this through the bottom hole of the next component. Thread one 6/0 bead and one 11/0 bead. Pick up the first component and take the elastic through the second 6/0, second 11/0 and third 6/0 bead of the former component. Thread one new 11/0 bead and one new 6/0 bead and run the elastic back through the top hole in the second component. Tie off as previously. Continue adding new components until the bracelet is the length you require, nine components for 7" and 10 components for an 8" bracelet.

3 Cut four pieces of 2" .012 mm flexible wire for each space between the components. Thread one strand through the first of the two center 6/0 beads, so the strand is one half on the top and one on the bottom of the bead, going from the left on top and the right on the bottom of the bead. With a second cord, go through the same bead at the opposite angle, going through the bead from right to left. This will form a crisscross of the two cords where they cross through the center of the bead. Put a dab of glue in the center of the bead to secure the strands and hold them in their correct location. Repeat this with the next two strands through the bottom bead, which is the next 6/0 bead in the center. You will now have four strands crisscrossing through the two large center beads where the two components connect. Repeat for all spaces around the bracelet.

4 Following the directions outlined in Step 7 for the necklace, add the wisps to each of the strands. Bend slightly and "fluff."

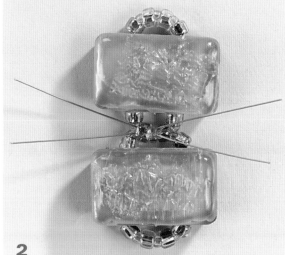

cat on a stone wall necklace

COMFORT

"Cats are intended to teach us that not everything in nature has a function." — Garrison Keillor

Designer: Susan Ray

Lampwork Artist: Amy Caswell

Finished Size: 18", without clasp

Expense: Less than $50

Level of Expertise: Stringing the necklace: Beginner; Lampwork: Advanced

Time to Complete: Stringing the necklace: One evening

supplies

1 happy cat 1¼" x 1½" lampwork focal bead

4 ruby red 10 mm lampwork beads

2 multi-tone 12 mm lampwork beads

4 cobalt blue 10 mm lampwork beads

4 celadon vintage acrylic 10 mm barrels

6 ruby red foil-lined 6/0 matte seed beads

2 citrine 6 mm round beads

6 stone-look ½" x 1" polymer barrels

24 silver 4 mm spacers

2 silver 4 mm disks

2 silver 6 mm disks

22" flexible wire

1 silver S-hook clasp with two 6 mm jump rings

2 sterling silver 2 mm x 3 mm crimp beads

tool box

Flat nose pliers

Wire cutters

Crimping pliers

tip — Amy's kitties come in a variety of sizes and poses. See the books "The Art and Soul of Glass Beads" and "Easy Beaded Jewelry" (KP Books) for other fine examples of her work!

Step-by-Step

1 See Basic Instructions, Single-Strand Necklace, page 146.

2 See Susan Ray's Basic Skewer Bead Instructions, page 137.

3 String beads as shown.

ice crystal ensemble

SOLITUDE

Designer: Susan Ray

Lampwork Artist: Gary Haun

Finished Sizes: Necklace: 16",
without clasp

Bracelet: 7", without clasp and
dangle

Earring Dangles: 1"

Expense: Over $50

Level of Expertise: Beginner

Time to Complete: One
evening

supplies

4 white-dot lampwork 12 mm x 7 mm discs

2 white-black lampwork 14 mm x 8 mm discs

4 white-black bumpy lampwork discs

2 white-peach bumpy lampwork discs

331 white frost 11/0 seed beads

78 white frost 6/0 seed beads

2 white frost 12 mm x 8 mm ovals

7 white frost 12 mm x 6 mm discs

6 peach satin 12 mm x 6 mm discs

8 sterling silver 2 mm x 3 mm crimp beads

1 sterling silver hook-and-eye clasp set

2 pieces of flexible wire: 19" and 22"

tool box

Flat nose pliers

Round nose pliers

Bead board

Wire cutters

Crimping pliers

necklace

3 frosted white 7 mm x 11 mm lampwork beads

4 frosted amber 7 mm x 11 mm lampwork beads

2 frosted white 9 mm x 14 mm bumpy lampwork beads

4 matte opaque black-white-dot frosted 12 mm x 16 mm bumpy lampwork beads

46 frosted white 6/0

28 matte black 11/0 seed beads

168 frosted white 13/0 seed beads

20" flexible wire

1 sterling silver toggle clasp

1 sterling silver 15 mm x 2 mm hollow star

1 sterling silver 6 mm jump ring

2 sterling silver 2 mm x 3 mm crimp beads

bracelet

3 frosted white 7 mm x 11 mm lampwork beads

2 frosted amber 7 mm x 11 mm lampwork beads

2 matte opaque white-dot frosted 9 mm x 14 mm lampwork beads

2 matte opaque black-white-dot frosted 10 mm x 15 mm lampwork beads

24 frosted white 6/0 seed beads

10 matte black 11/0 seed beads

20 frosted white 13/0 seed beads

11" flexible wire

1 sterling silver toggle clasp

1 sterling silver 15 mm x 2 mm hollow star

1 sterling silver 6 mm jump ring

2 sterling silver 2 mm x 3 mm crimp beads

earring dangles

2 white-dot etched 12 mm x 8 mm
lampwork beads

4 matte black 11/0 seed beads

4 frosted white 13/0 seed beads

4 frosted white 6/0

2 frosted white 10 mm x 8 mm ovals

2 sterling silver 3" head pins

2 sterling silver earring wires

 tip *There is no need to lay out your seed beads. Lay out your large beads on your bead board and string on seed beads as you go.*

Step-by-Step

1 *See Basic Instructions, Single-Strand Necklace, page 146; Single-Strand Bracelet, page 147; Earrings, page 154.*

 "I enjoy encasing my beads in clear glass, allowing them to capture and reflect light in unexpected ways."
— *Gary Haun*

FYI: *Modern, handmade glass beads are called lampwork or perle a lume. This term denotes the "lamp" or flame used to make the beads. In past generations, this work also was called "wound" work to describe the technique of "wounding" a drop of molten glass around a steel mandrel while in the flame. Lampwork is an age-old process with techniques hidden for centuries. Today's marketplace and the Internet allow open access to these techniques.*

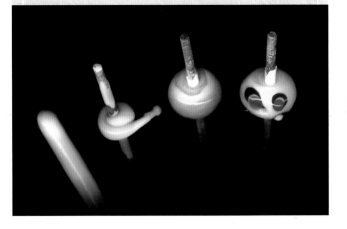

desert blooms bracelet

TIMELESS

"That we find a crystal or a poppy beautiful means that we are less alone, that we are more deeply inserted into existence than the course of a single life would lead us to believe." — *John Berger*

Designer: Sue Kwong and Karen Li

Lampwork Artist: Karen Leonardo

Finished Size: 7½" long

Expense: More than $100

Level of Expertise: Advanced

Time to Complete: One day

supplies

1 antique turquoise 11 mm x 22 mm nugget

3 AB 8 mm rounds

12 deep amethyst 4 mm cubes

5 lampwork 19 mm beads

3 Bali sterling silver 12 mm beads

4 yellow lampwork 7 mm spacers

4 orange lampwork 7 mm spacers

2 turquoise lampwork 7 mm spacers

16 Swarovski turquoise 3 mm bicones

19 sterling silver 4 mm spacers

1 Swarovski green 10 mm bicone

1 Swarovski light green 10 mm bicone

1 Swarovski orange 10 mm bicone

1 Swarovski pink 10 mm bicone

1 Swarovski lavender 10 mm bicone

6 white 8 mm freshwater pearls

6 turquoise 6 mm rounds

6 sterling silver 6 mm bead caps

1 sterling silver 17 mm square photo charm

1 sterling silver square toggle clasp

19 sterling silver 24-gauge head pins

36" sterling silver 22-gauge wire

tool box

Chain nose pliers

Round nose pliers

Wire cutters

Ruler

Step-by-Step

1 There are seven sections in this bracelet, four sections of lampwork beads and three sections of Bali sterling silver beads. Each section is made and linked together using the wrapped loop method *(see Wrapped Loop Method Instructions, page 152)*. Cut a piece of 22-gauge sterling silver wire 3" long for each section.

2 For the focal lampwork bead section, use one Swarovski turquoise crystal three mm bicone, one lampwork 7 mm spacer (choose appropriate colors for the lampwork) one focal lampwork bead, one lampwork 7 mm spacer, and one Swarovski turquoise crystal 3 mm bicone. For the Bali sterling silver bead sections, use one sterling silver 4 mm spacer, one Bali sterling silver 12 mm bead, and one sterling silver 4 mm spacer.

3 Starting with the Bali sterling silver bead section, attach one Bali sterling silver bead section to one focal lampwork bead section with the wrapped loop method. Finish with Bali sterling silver bead section. You now have five sections linked together. Two focal lampwork bead sections are attached in the next step.

4 Make a loop with your sterling silver wire. Open loop, attach to one Bali sterling silver bead section. Close loop and wrap loops. String on crystal, lampwork spacer, lampwork bead, lampwork spacer and crystal, make loop, open loop, attach the square toggle, close loop and wrap. Using head pin, string on one focal lampwork bead section, attach to square toggle using the wrapped loop method. You now have one end with a toggle clasp complete.

5 Complete the other bracelet end: Cut a piece of wire 3" long, make loop, open loop, attach to the end focal lampwork bead section and the photo charm. String on one sterling silver 3 mm spacer bead, make loop, open loop, attach the male part of the toggle clasp, close loop and wrap. You now have completed the body of the bracelet.

6 Make dangles: Dangles are all made using head pins. There are three different dangles between each section; pearl and crystal dangle, sterling silver spacer and turquoise dangle, and Bali sterling silver bead caps and large Swarovski crystal dangle. Using head pins, make 18 dangles and attach to the bracelet *(see Dangle Instructions, page 154)*.

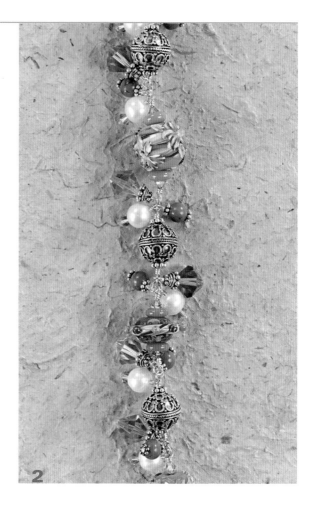

rain forest
parrot necklace

ENCHANTING

"Trees are the Earth's endless effort to speak to the listening heaven."
— Rabindranath Tagore

Designer: Susan Ray

Lampwork Artist: Rebecca Jurgens

Finished Size: 22", without clasp or hanging 2¾" pendant

Expense: $50 - $100

Level of Expertise: Stringing the necklace: Beginner

Time to Complete: One evening

supplies

1 parrot (2¾" long) lampwork pendant

2 floral 16 mm lampwork beads

2 ruby red 12 mm lampwork beads

4 red-pink 12 mm accent lampwork beads

139 ruby red 6/0 beads

28 gold 6/0 bells

7 antique turquoise 6 mm round

4 antique turquoise 8 mm round

1 ruby red glass 6 mm round

1 crystal 4 mm bicone

1 ruby red 13/0 foil-lined seed bead, to act as a stop

30" flexible wire

1 goldtone toggle clasp

2 brass 2 mm x 3 mm crimp beads

tool box

Flat nose pliers

Wire cutters

Crimping pliers

Step-by-Steps

See Single-Strand Basic Instructions, pages 146-150.

1 String one half of your beads.

2 Add the pendant: String a 13/0 ruby red seed bead, 6/0 transparent red seed bead, a 6 mm antique turquoise bead, the pendant, and the 8 mm gold crow through the 5" head pin. Create a loop at the top, close to the crow, and add one red 13/0 seed bead to act as a stop. Bring your flexible wire around the 13/0 seed bead and back through the crow, turquoise pendant and 8 mm red bead. *(See Dangle Instructions, page 154.)* String on pendant.

3 String the remainder of the beads on the other half of your necklace. Attach the clasp.

 tip *If you want the opportunity to remove the pendant later, use a jump ring to attach the pendant to the necklace.*

BASICS

chapter 6

"It is not so much for its beauty that the forest makes a claim upon men's hearts, as for that subtle something, that quality of air, that emanation from old trees, that so wonderfully changes and renews a weary spirit." — Robert Louis Stevenson

susan ray's skewer beads

supplies

½ ounce of any color of Sculpey PREMO! polymer clay

1 wooden skewer

1 plastic work sheet (dedicated to polymer clay)

1 flat-blade cutter

1 pasta machine (dedicated to polymer clay)

1 toaster oven (dedicated to polymer clay)

Optional: 1 sculpting tool with wooden handle

Optional: 1 extra-large emery board

Optional: Sculpey Satin or Gloss Glaze

Ruler

I created this technique myself. I am sure that the idea originated in my mother's kitchen at some time or another, but for now, polymer is the medium!

Don't shortcut CONDITIONING. Your beads will not harden if the clay is not properly conditioned. The polymer compounds need to be mixed, before baking, so the clay can harden to the proper consistency. Knead away!

Many polymer artists set aside time to "condition" clay by rolling it over and over through their pasta machines, then placing it in plastic bags for use when their creative juices are flowing.

creating SKEWER polymer beads

Skewer beads are made two ways: the LUMP method or SLAB method. For beginners, the LUMP method is a good starting point. Once you get the concept, you will want the additional control you get from the SLAB method.

1 To create your first skewer base, take a lump of clay that is approximately ½ ounce in weight. It doesn't matter what color clay you use for your initial project. The idea is to get used to using this technique to make polymer beads.

2 Pre-condition the clay by rolling through the pasta machine at least 15 times (Check manufacturer's directions for conditioning clay.)

3 Roll the clay between your hands until it resembles a barrel shape, approx. ½" in diameter and 1½" in length.

4 Place the skewer through the middle of the clay's short end.

5 Pull the lump to the middle of the skewer, being careful to keep the skewer in the center of the clay.

6 Try to retain the barrel shape as you move the clay up the skewer.

7 Roll the clay on the skewer as you would roll out clay to make a snake. Use a clean, dry work surface that is dedicated to your polymer work. My work surface is an old Tupperware pie crust rolling mat.

8 Make the clay at least twice the length of the original, at least ¼" in diameter and 7" in length by rolling along the work surface. Apply even pressure.

9 If the clay wall becomes too thin to work with (you must maintain at least ⅛" in thickness for beads) use your thumbs and forefingers to draw the clay back towards the center of the skewer and re-roll.

10 Allow your new tube of beads to rest before cutting, just as you would with a new cane. I usually wait at least one hour.

11 After you have used the skewer a few times, it will be coated with some of the polymer clay and the beads will no longer easily pull away from the skewer surface. Once this happens, discard the skewer and start anew.

12 Cutting your beads: For this first example we will use a ruler as the mark to cut the beads. Lay down your skewer next to a ruler edge and place a small slice (using your blade cutter) across the top of the skewered snake at each 1" mark. Now place the skewer in one hand, and using your blade cutter, complete the cut. It is helpful to start at one end.

13 Rotate the skewer and the clay to get an even cut all the way around. This takes some practice. Don't be discouraged if your first cuts are uneven. Using your blade, even up the ends. The beads may not all be a consistent size at this stage, but hey, you made a very fine bead, didn't you?

14 Once the first bead is cut, remove it from the skewer and tap each end onto the flat side of the blade cutter. This will help to even out your cut and give the ends a flat, consistent and professional appearance. Check for bad cuts. Sometimes a small sliver of clay will remain that needs attention. Massage it back into the clay body or cut it away. (If at first you don't succeed, remove your clay from the skewer and start again.) Now we're having fun!

15 You also can create a slight "well" in the ends of the bead by using a sculpting tool. Remove a bead from the skewer. Take your sculpting tool and place one end within the hole of the bead. Apply ever-so-slight pressure on the end and the well will form naturally as the wooden handle of the tool meets the clay.

16 Once all the beads are cut to perfection, bake following manufacturer's directions. I use Sculpey PREMO! clay exclusively and prefer to bake my beads in a toaster oven at 275 degrees for 20 to 30 minutes, depending on their size. Place your beads directly onto the toaster-oven pan or suspend them on a bicycle spoke. Either method works well. (Sometimes a shiny edge will appear where the clay touched the pan. Use an emery board to remove the shine.)

17 It is important to allow your beads to cool in the oven.

18 If you wish to add a glaze finish or just want to clean up the beads, I recommend buying extra large emery boards. These are simple and easy to use. I often sit with a pot of beads in my lap while watching TV and sand them to a fine finish using a single emery board.

19 Most of my beads remain in their natural soft-shine state. However, some designers prefer to add more shine. Apply your finishing glaze as directed by the manufacturer. I use Sculpey Satin Glaze or Sculpey Gloss Glaze for my beads.

NEVER use your kitchen utensils, oven or supplies when working with polymer clay. ALWAYS have a separate set of tools just for clay work.

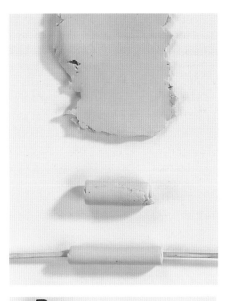

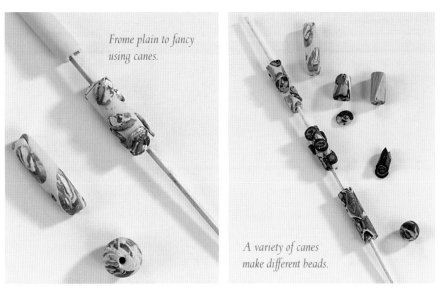

Frome plain to fancy using canes.

A variety of canes make different beads.

Advanced cane application.

SLAB method skewer base

The SLAB method for making skewer beads takes a little more time but provides better control of the diameter of the beads.

1 Begin with a lump of clay that is approximately ½ ounce of weight.

2 Set your pasta machine on the thickest setting.

3 Pre-condition the clay by rolling through the pasta machine at least 15 times. Be sure to check manufacturer's directions regarding conditioning. Each clay body MUST be conditioned.

Skewers come in two convenient sizes. The smaller 10" skewer is ideal for small delicate beads, while the larger 12" skewer works wonders for bulky nuggets and larger beads. I find skewers in plastic packs at a local discount store.

Types of skewer beads which can be made by this method.

4 Continue to fold the clay in half, inserting the folded edge first through the machine until you have created a 2" x 4" slab.

5 Lay the wooden skewer lengthwise over one edge of the clay. Roll the clay onto the skewer creating your snake. Gently tap seam in place.

6 Roll the clay out on your work sheet as stated in Step 7 for LUMP method skewer beads on page 137. Continue to follow the directions for the LUMP method.

adding embellishments

The most fun in making skewer beads is the ease with which you can add embellishments. You can roll the skewered clay through glitter and herbs to add inclusions or make interesting color combination canes — slice off the thinnest cane and apply to the skewer clay. Once you are happy with your inclusions, simply roll gently along your work surface.

Use of inclusions is fun. BE SAFE too! Some inclusions may be flammable. Take care to use only inclusions that will not start a fire when you bake your beads in your toaster oven. ALWAYS — safety first.

making variegated colors

1 Now try the SLAB technique, as above, to create the variegated effects of malachite, jasper and other natural stones. This time begin with ½ ounce each of two different colors.

2 Condition each color in the pasta machine 15 times on the thickest setting.

3 Make two balls (one of each color).

4 Turn the balls into snakes by rolling each ball out onto your work sheet until it resembles a snake.

5 Twist the snakes together. Roll the twisted snake through the pasta machine (on thickest setting) folding the clay in half and running the folded edge through the pasta machine first until you are happy with the variegation. This should take only four or five passes through the pasta machine making a 2" x 6" slab. Roll your slab onto a skewer and roll even. Cut barrels as desired.

6 You will have a variegated pattern of the two colors.

forming round beads

supplies

½ ounce of any color of Sculpey PREMO! polymer clay

1 wooden skewer

1 plastic work sheet (dedicated to polymer clay)

1 flat-blade cutter

Ruler

1 pasta machine (dedicated to polymer clay)

1 toaster oven (dedicated to polymer clay)

Scrap clay

You easily can make round beads with precision using this skewer method.

1 Make sure your tube (rolled out onto a skewer) is even in diameter.

2 Lay a ruler along the side of the skewer.

3 Using a gentle hand, make a slight slice along the top edge of the tube at the desired length. I began by making 1" beads.

4 Lift the skewer away from the ruler and use the slices as a guide to cut away each bead.

5 Once the beads are cut, allow to rest while you make the inner "balls of clay" from scrap clay.

6 Make a ¼" diameter x 3" snake of scrap clay. Cut the pieces into ¼" lengths.

7 Roll the pieces into small balls.

8 Cut open, lengthwise, each tube of clay made on your skewers.

9 Place the small ball of clay inside the newly created opening and fold the outside surface of the clay over it until you cannot see any of the inner surface.

10 Manipulate the clay between your fingers until a new ball is formed.

11 Use a skewer to pierce the surface and create a hole for your bead. Make sure both sides of the bead have equal size holes.

forming a pendant from a round bead

Once you have made round beads, it is very easy to create round pendants!

1 Make several round beads approximately 1" in diameter.

2 Place your bead on your work surface. Using your palm as a form, cup the bead with your hand.

3 Gently apply pressure over the bead until it begins to flatten.

4 To maintain the roundness of the original bead, do not flatten completely.

5 Cut a ¼" length of non-tarnish or precious metal wire. Bend the wire over a skewer.

6 Insert the ends of the newly formed "U" into one edge of the pendant. Bake as directed by manufacturer.

bead size chart

Metric is the name of the game when it comes to beads. Beads come from all over the world and since the metric system is used elsewhere, beads are measured in millimeters more often than not. If you never were a fan of metric, here are simple charts to help you make the transition. Be sure to keep your chart handy when buying beads online. Photos can often distort the size of a bead. Be sure to read the fine print when purchasing beads online or in catalogs.

How many beads make a 16" strand?

Approximately:
- 2 mm = 203 beads
- 3 mm = 136 beads
- 4 mm = 100 beads
- 6 mm = 67 beads
- 8 mm = 50 beads
- 10 mm = 41 beads
- 12 mm = 34 beads

Bugle Bead Sizes

1 2 3 5

Millimeter/ Inch Gauge

mm inches

Size	
7/0	
8/0	
9/0	
10/0	
11/0	
12/0	
14/0	
16/0	
20/0	

Square MM Sizes

- 3 x 3 mm
- 4 x 4 mm
- 5 x 5 mm

Seed Beads Per Inch

Use these approximate counts of seed beads per inch to help plan your own designs

Bead Size	Beads per inch
11/0	20
8/0	12
5/0	7

Oval Bead Sizes in Millimeters

- 6 x 4
- 7 x 5
- 8 x 6
- 10 x 8
- 12 x 10
- 14 x 10
- 16 x 12

Round Bead Sizes in Millimeters

- 2 mm
- 3 mm
- 4 mm
- 5 mm
- 6 mm
- 7 mm
- 8 mm
- 9 mm
- 10 mm
- 11 mm
- 12 mm
- 14 mm
- 16 mm
- 18 mm

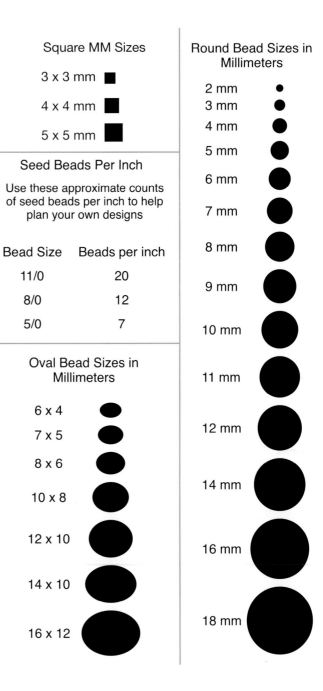

storing your beads

The nice thing about beading as a hobby is that the beads and tools are compact and easy to store, but organization is a must.

If you are organized and store your materials close at hand, you will be able to spend more time enjoying your hobby, rather than searching for what you need.

organize your space

1 A table or desk with a chair that is the correct height for you is essential.

2 The work surface itself should be large enough to lay out your bead board, tools and bead box.

3 Very good lighting is critical. A portable, true-color lamp is an excellent choice. It shows the colors and details of the beads, is great for color matching and reduces eye fatigue.

Use secure containers to keep beads and supplies from being a temptation to small children or pets. If you have cats, it's a good idea to cover your work area with a bath towel or blanket.

take it with you

Tackle boxes or portable toolboxes are very handy. They can hold small bead containers, as well as trays and stringing supplies. Always look for plastic storage containers where the dividers are permanently affixed and the lid closes flush to the top of the dividers. This way, when the unit is raised for carrying, no beads will migrate and mix.

basic toolbox

Once you have your fabulous beads in hand, there are only a few tools and basic materials required to complete a wonderful project.

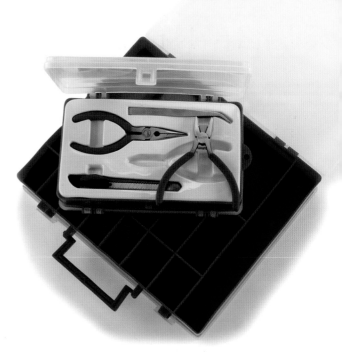

standard tools

Wire cutters	True-color light
Flat nose pliers	Various glues
Needle nose or round nose pliers	Storage containers
Journal for inspiration	Ruler
Bead board	Hemostats

There are only a few types of tools to consider when beading: cutters, pliers, and crimpers. With so few tools to get you on your way, make the most of your dollar. Look for tools that provide easy handling, such as those that are anti-glare and have sure-grip, ergo handles.

Choosing the right set of tools can seem daunting. Here is a checklist that might assist you. Consider the following:

• Price

• Comfortable fit in your hand

• Small enough blades for extremely detailed work

• Strength of the blades

• Anti-glare finish to prevent eye fatigue

• Spring tension for ease of use

• Resistance to rust in a humid climate

what tools to buy

journal

Carry a journal and colored pencils to retain ideas. Sometimes, in setting out your beads, you will stumble onto more than one great pattern. It is a good idea to write down or draw your ideas for use on another project at a later time.

bead board

Most bead boards have rulers. The three- and four-channel trays provide a wide variety of uses. Always use the outermost channel when making a one-strand bracelet or necklace. The channels closer to the middle of the board are not an accurate measurement.

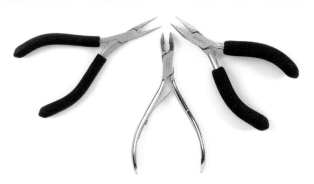

The most basic of tools needed include, from left: a round nose pliers, wire cutter and a flat nose pliers (also called a chain nose pliers).

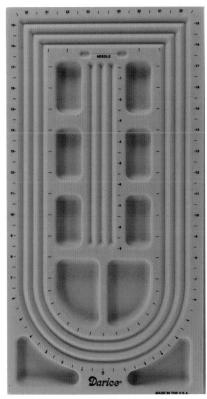

Three-channel bead board

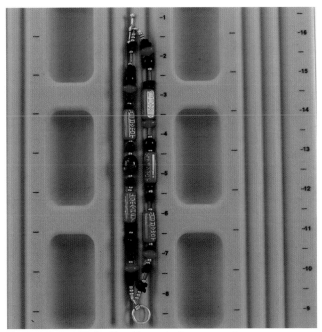

The bead board has a ruler for easy measuring.

start by stringing

Making a simple one-strand bracelet with a flexible wire and toggle clasp closure is a good way to begin beadwork. If you have worked with hemp, elastic or memory wire before, you will enjoy the more finished look that metal closures and flexible wire can bring.

By designer Sandi Webster

single-strand basics

crimps

What size crimp beads? Crimp bead sizes, material and color are a personal preference, but I have found 2 mm x 3 mm sterling silver crimps hold the best and will not loosen after months (or years) of wear. Use only precious metal crimps. Sterling silver crimps are more flexible, respond easily to flattening and hold up well.

wire

Use the best flexible wire you can find. Beadalon is strong and pliable. It comes in a number of colors, diameters and strengths. Try 7-strand .018-gauge silver-gray Beadalon for most of the projects in this book. If you encounter difficulty in finding any of the products recommended, see the Resources listing, page 160.

making a bracelet

Most women have wrist sizes from 6½" to 8". If you are making a bracelet for yourself, use another bracelet from your jewelry case as your guide.

Also consider the size of the beads in your design. If your beads are extra large, their girth will take up extra room, as the bracelet will rest above the wrist instead of on it. So, when working with extra large beads, compensate for their size by adding some length.

basic bracelet materials

Assorted beads: Gather 20 to 30 beads for a bracelet. You will need 60 or more beads for a necklace, depending on their shape (with an average size of 6 mm).

Bead board: Use one that will comfortably meet the needs of the size of your design, as well as your available work area.

Containers: Use a divided storage container, muffin tin or small jars for sorting beads.

7-strand .018-gauge silver-gray flexible wire: How much wire? A good rule of thumb is 12" for a standard single-strand bracelet and one yard for the longest of necklaces, lariats or eyeglass holders. For a necklace and bracelet set, plan on using one yard. It is better to error on the side of more wire than less. When crimping an end that is short on wire, the task can get pretty labor-intensive. So, in this instance, more is better.

Toggle or lobster clasp: Use a toggle set or lobster claw clasp with tab end in gold, silver, base metal, pewter or vermeil. (If the tab end is not available, use a jump ring or a split ring instead.) Be careful when using base metal or pewter toggles; the metal is so soft it can sometimes be broken.

"Jewelry making is such fun. Don't spoil your fun by demanding perfection of yourself. The goal is to have a finished piece of jewelry that was handmade by you; one of a kind. You want to impress people with your ability to make a piece of jewelry/art, not produce a piece that looks like machined perfection." — Roberta Ogborn

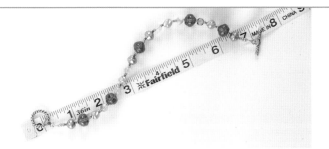

single-strand bracelet

1 Measure your wrist and cut 12" of flexible wire from the spool.

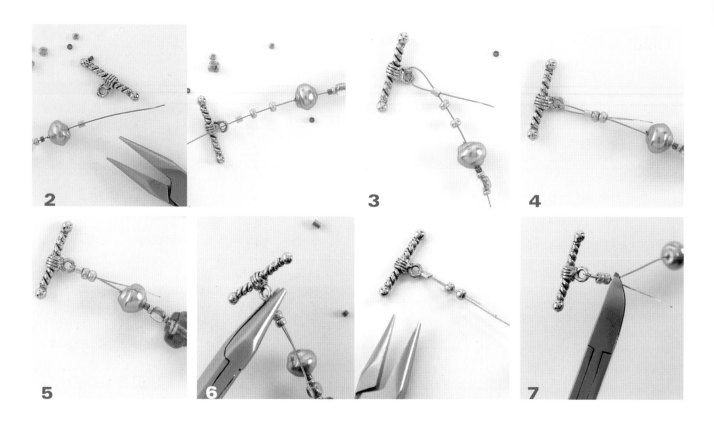

2 To add the clasp to one end, string on the crimp bead on one end of the wire, allowing it to slide 1" from the end, and then string on one end of the clasp.

3 Hold the crimp bead in place and loop the end of flexible wire back through the crimp bead. Allow 1" of wire to pass through the crimp bead.

4 Take end through first two beads on the strand.

5 Pull the crimp beads up tight to the clasp.

6 With flat nose pliers, cover the crimp bead entirely and press down firmly to flatten the crimp bead. Spin the crimp bead around and press down firmly again. Your crimp bead should be uniformly flattened on both sides. Test the closure by pulling firmly on the wire to be sure the crimp bead will hold.

7 Use wire cutters to clip off the excess from the shorter wire end and discard the clipped piece.

8

10

11

13

8 String on beads as desired. The first few beads on either end of your bracelet must have large enough holes to accommodate both strands of wire (so avoid ending with seed beads). These beads must be small enough to easily fit through a toggle closure. Try using 6/0 or 8/0 beads for ending, if possible. As you work, check to be sure that your short wire has remained strung within the first few beads and that no beads are "hung up" on the wire.

9 Finish the strand as you began, followed by the crimp bead and clasp.

10 Loop the end of the wire back through the crimp.

11 Snug the crimp and two end beads close to the toggle, pulling on the end to tighten any gaps of wire in the design. Be sure to string through clasp, crimp and metal beads or other beads all at once.

12 Once the short wire has been pulled as far as possible, hold the bracelet vertically with the finished end down. Make sure no space remains between any of the beads. Check again for proper fit on your wrist before crimping.

13 Flatten the crimp and cut the wire, as in Steps 7 and 8 for the first end.

The finished bracelet.

single-strand necklace tips

The steps are the same as a single-strand bracelet except for the length of the finished piece. Use the steps below to determine the length for your necklace.

1 To determine the size of your finished necklace, choose the length you want from choker to longer necklace.

2 If you are making a choker, measure your neck with a string at the position you want the necklace to rest.

3 Add 1" to your neck measurement for the correct size of your finished piece.

4 Take the desired finished necklace length and add 4" to determine the length of wire to cut.

By designer Jessica Italia

making a multi-strand bracelet

To complete a multi-strand bracelet with equal length strands, repeat the instructions specified in the Single-Strand Step-by-Step section on pages 147 to 149, for each strand of the bracelet, completing one strand at a time.

Use the how-to photos on page 151 for additional guidance, if necessary, as you finish the second strand.

By designer Sandi Webster

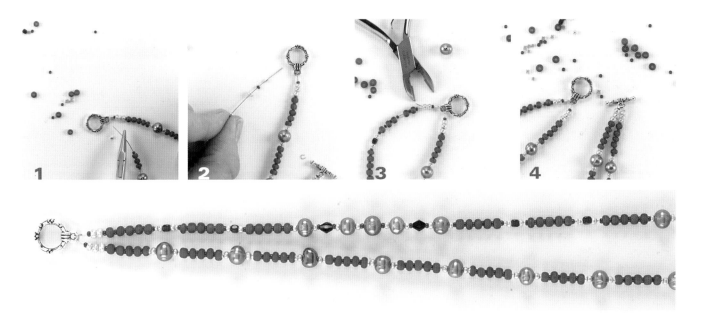

By designer Nora Howe. Lampwork Artist: Karen Leonardo.

1 Use hemostats to hold the end of the second beaded strand.

2 Finish the strand with small beads and the crimp bead.

3 Loop wire through the clasp and back through the crimp and first three beads on the strand, just as with the first strand.

4 Finish as before, by pulling the crimp snug to the clasp, checking the length around your wrist, flattening the crimp bead on both sides and snipping the excess wire tail.

Completing multi-strand necklace or choker, is as easy as the single strand! Just following the same steps twice. *See Basic Stringing, Single Strand, pages 146-149.* The only difference is determining what style necklace you'd like (same length, graduated strands or torsade) and then cutting each wire strand accordingly. A multi-channel bead board will help you determine the number of beads in each strand.

simple wrapped loop method

By Eileen Feldman

supplies

1 roll of 20- to 24-gauge wire*

*Practice with copper, brass, or other base metal wire before moving onto sterling silver. (See Resources, page 160, for Artistic Wire. Sterling silver is available from Rio Grande.)

tool box

Round nose pliers

Flat nose pliers

Wire cutters

Step-by-Step

1 Cut a piece of wire approximately 1½" longer than desired finished length.

2 Bend one end of the wire at a 90-degree angle close to the end of the bead using a flat nose pliers.

3 Using a round nose pliers, wrap the wire around the pliers making a small loop.

4 Cut away excess wire with wire cutter. Optional: Add jump ring.

5 Close loop using flat nose pliers.

6 String on desired beads leaving 1" of remaining wire.

7 Bend wire to 90-degree angle using flat nose pliers.

8 Use round nose pliers to form a second loop.

9 Cut away excess wire. Add additional jump ring.

10 Close the loop and attached jump ring with round nose pliers.

11 Continue to add lengths of wire by forming new loops and attaching to next section by jump ring.

12 You also can add your clasp to the length using the attached jump rings as connectors.

By Sandi Webster

closures

toggles

Toggles are a favorite style for bracelets. A toggle is very easy to fasten with just one hand. Toggle clasps can be tricky when attaching multiple strands. Be sure that the bar-end of the toggle can fit comfortably through the ring with the beads on the strand.

When choosing a necklace clasp, be sure it is secure for the weight or number of strands. Also consider how it will feel on the back of the neck.

button-and-loop

One interesting, inexpensive closure can be made from a shank button and a beaded loop. Here's how to start stringing your piece with a button-loop closure:

1 Cut the desired length of wire and thread a crimp bead onto it.

2 Thread on an odd number of seed beads. The length that the seed beads cover the wire should equal ¼" more than the diameter of the button you are using. This will allow the button to slide through the loop.

3 After you have threaded the appropriate number of seed beads, thread your wire back through the crimp.

4 Pull on both wires together, as you push the crimp toward the loop of seed beads to remove any slack.

The finished loop.

The finished button end.

5 Flatten the crimp.

6 String your strand as usual, covering your tail of wire next to the crimp with two or three beads.

7 On the other end, attach the button just as you would any other clasp.

earrings and dangles basics

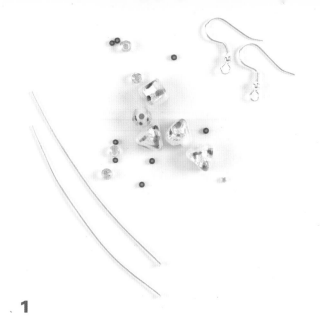

Learning to make earrings is easy and it's a quick jewelry project. The basic component for making earrings is a dangle. The technique used to make dangles is learning how to "twist" the wire at the top, which is sometimes called a rosary turn or wrapped loop.

Use only sterling silver or other precious metal headpins when making earrings. You will be frustrated if you try to use base metal pins. Even experienced designers find that base metal does not make for a good turn. Practice makes perfect!

1

making earrings

Step-by-Step

Let's begin with a dangle that is prepared first and then added to your earrings or necklace later. You will need sterling or vermeil headpins in 2" to 4" lengths.

Although some can comfortably make this turn with 2" headpins, you may prefer 3" to 4" lengths. It is easier to learn to make a dangle "off-line" when learning this technique. Once you have the technique down, you can actually do them directly onto the earring wires or necklace.

toolbox

Round nose or needle nose pliers

Sharp wire cutters (for cutting sterling silver wire)

Flat nose pliers

❀ tip   *The smaller, more delicate the cone on the round nose pliers, the more delicate the results will be on the turn.*

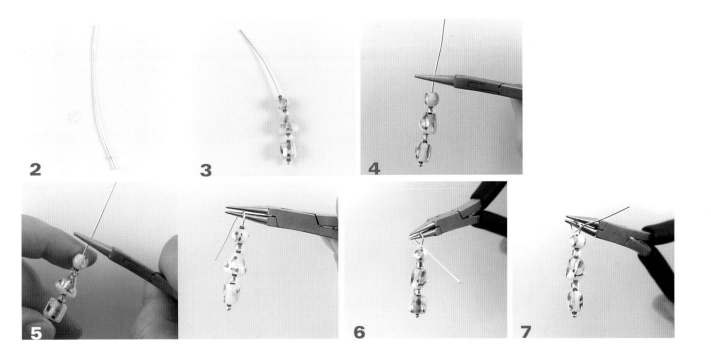

2

3

4

5

6

7

1 Assemble the items needed for your earrings: two headpins, two ear wires and enough beads to make matching patterns on both of the dangles.

2 String the beads onto the headpin using the tiny head of the pin as the base of the dangle. If your first bead is too large and falls off the head of the pin, add a small transparent 10/0 or 11/0 seed bead or a 2 mm to 3 mm silver or gold bead on the end first. This will help hold the larger bead in place.

3 Stop adding beads when you have approximately 1" (or more) of the pin showing.

4 Place your round nose pliers approximately ¼" from the top of the last bead. Grasp the pin tightly with the pliers.

5 Using your thumb and forefinger, bend the wire over the back of your pliers.

6 Cross the wire underneath and in front of the stationary wire, forming the start of the loop.

7 Bring the wire forward, beginning the first complete turn.

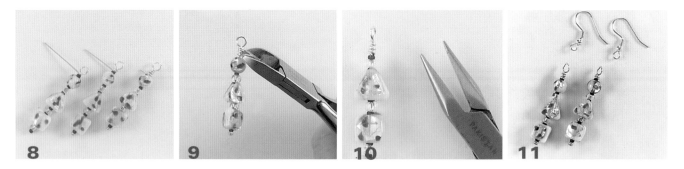

8 Grasp the newly formed loop with the pliers and turn the loop several times to provide three neatly spaced turns. Some people choose to turn the wire instead of the loop, but we have had the best results by turning the loop itself. This seems to give a more precise finish to the work.

9 When the turns are completed, cut away the remainder of the wire.

10 Grasping the loop, tuck the newly cut end down and in toward the top bead with your flat nose pliers.

11 Now your dangle is complete and can be strung onto the earring wire.

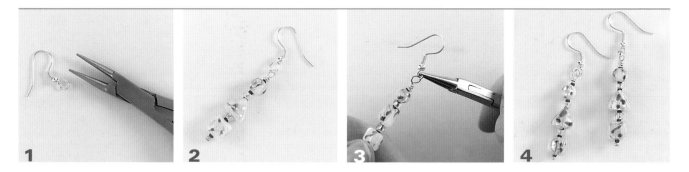

adding on the ear wires

When making earrings, complete your dangles first. Be sure they match by holding them side by side. Place them on an ear wire that opens by following these steps:

1 With round nose pliers, gently open the loop on the ear wire by twisting it slightly to the side. Try opening at the front or back of the loop. Do not pull it apart, as it will be very difficult to close.

2 Slide on your dangle.

3 Close the loop with the round nose pliers.

4 To regain symmetry, press the loop gently between blades of a flat nose pliers for the finished look, as shown.

Once you have accomplished the turn, you should practice doing this directly onto the loop of a pair of French ear wires. To do so, "thread" the French ear wire loop onto the headpin before you bend the loop down and forward. Once the earring loop is in place, keep it out of the way while you complete the turns.

about the photographer

MINIMAL

"Just living is not enough... One must have sunshine, freedom, and a little flower."
— *Hans Christian Andersen*

For the past several years, Galena, Illinois resident, Richard B. Pearce, Ph.D. has been developing a high-resolution digital method aimed at capturing broad, detailed, close-up images of native upper Mississippi flora and insects. Because the lens and light source both move across the subject during exposure, a true digital *scan* is made without film or a camera. The technique eliminates many of the artifacts that detract from conventional close-up photography: a blurred periphery, an exceedingly narrow focal depth and a limited field of view. Perhaps most importantly, the image resolution bridges the gap between close-up photography and microscopy. That means it's possible to resolve individual pollen grains or see striations on a butterfly's tongue!

DESIGNERS

Irene Baranowitz
Creative Spirit
1953 Lakebrook Circle
Dandridge, TN 37725
(865) 397-3880
E-mail: ibaran@comcast.net
Website: www.ezcraft.com

Tracy Callahan
Rubber Stamps of Arkansas
1611 West Bradley Lane
Russellville, AR 72801
(479) 968-1926
E-mail: Tracyc@cox-internet.com
Website: www.rubberstampsofarkansas.com

Amy Caswell
Caswell Glass Studios
173 S. Ventu Park Road
Newbury Park, CA 91320
(805) 499-0707
E-mail: beads@caswellstudios.com
Website: www.caswellstudios.com

Eileen Feldman
Eileen Feldman Designs
36-04 Berdan Ave.
Fair Lawn, NJ 07410
(201) 321-6583
E-mail: eileensf@optonline.net
Website: www.eileenfeldmandesigns.net

Gary Haun
1650 Little Fishtrap Road
Lawrenceburg, TN 38464
(931) 722-9164
E-mail: garyh@netease.net

Jeanne Holland
Vintaj
704 Park Ave.
Galena, IL 61036
(815) 541-5558
E-mail: Jeanne@karmul.com
Website: www.vintaj.com / www.karmul.com

syndee holt
Polyform Products/Jacquard Products
Polyform: (847) 427-0020
Jacquard: (800) 442-0455
E-mail: syndeeh@msn.com
Website: www.sculpey.com; www.jacquardproducts.com

Jessica Italia
The Bead Bar
109 N. Main St.
Galena, IL 61036
(815) 777-4080
E-mail: GalenaBeadBar@msn.com
Website: www.GalenaBeadBar.com

Rebecca Jurgens
L&S Arts
7953 NE Sunnywoods Lane
Kingston, WA 98346
(360) 297-8676
E-mail: landsart1@aol.com

Patricia Kimle
Patricia Kimle Designs
E-mail: patti@kimledesigns.com
Website: www.kimledesigns.com

Tamara A. Knight
Knight Beads (Wholesale Only)
32 Windwood Drive
Aurora, IL 60506
(630) 466-0979
E-mail: Knightbeads@aol.com

Sue Kwong and Karen Li
2310 S. Eighth Ave.
Arcadia, CA 91006
(626) 574-3186
E-mail: heartbeads@adelphia.net

Lynn Larkins
Lynnier Concepts
228 S. First St., Suite 202
Milwaukee, WI 53204-1477
(414) 765-0200
Fax: (414) 765-1350
E-mail: lynnierconcepts@iopener.net

Karen J. Leonardo
Just Leonardo
362 Hood School Road
Indiana, PA 15701
(724) 357-8709
E-mail: justleao7@ptd.net
Website: www.justleonardo.com

Barbara Markoe
Rituals Jewelry
10668 Ranch Road
Culver City, CA 98230
(310) 202-7807
E-mail: ritualsjewelry@comcast.net
Website: www.ritualsjewelry.com
eBay Seller ID: ritualsjewelr

Wendy Mullane
Vintaj
704 Park Ave.
Galena, IL 61036
(815) 541-0219
E-mail: wmullane@karmul.com
Website: www.vintaj.com; www.karmul.com

Roberta Ogborn
iamtrappedinabead
5905 Stephanie Drive
Milton, FL 32570
(850) 983-7265
E-mail: obobbio@msn.com
Website: www.iamtrappedinabead.homestead.com

Susan Ray
18098 Fulton Road
Maquoketa, IA 52060
(563) 652-3307
E-mail: raysa524@aol.com

Marie Segal
Clay Factory Inc.
P.O. Box 46059
Escondido, CA 92046-0598
E-mail: marie@clayfactoryinc.com
Website: www.clayfactoryinc.com

Cynthia Vela
Eye Candy
16331 Brush Meadow
Sugarland, TX 77478
(281) 277-2939
E-mail: cindyvela@hotmail.com

Sandi Webster
Zara Designs
5217 Old Spicewood Spg Rg.
Austin, TX 78731
(512) 794-9335
E-mail: rwebster1@austin.rr.com
Website: www.zaradesigns.com
eBay seller ID: designsbysandi

Nancy Ellen Wolfe
New Designs
130 River Landing Drive
Charleston, SC 29492
(843) 345-8585
E-mail: jewelry@newolfedesigns.com

RESOURCES

Arrow Springs
4301 Product Drive
Shingle Springs, CA 95682
(530) 677-1400
Web site: www.arrowsprings.com

Artistic Wire
Elmhurst, IL 60126
Web site: www.artisticwire.com

Clay Factory Inc.
Marie Segal
P.O. Box 460598
Escondido, CA 92046-0598
(760) 741-3242
(877) 728-5739
Web site: www.clayfactoryinc.com

Crystal Cottage Studio

Crystal Cottage Studio
Shelly Penko
3664 Ridgeland Road
West Bloomfield, MI 48323
(248) 855-2989
E-mail: shelly@crystalcottagestudio.com
E-mail: penko@crystalcottagestudio.com
Web site: www.crystalcottagestudio.com
eBay user ID: crystalcottage

Faux Dichro
Creative Spirit Crafts
2354 Chapman Highway
Sevierville, TN 37725
(800) 311-6529

Fire Mountain Gems
1 Fire Mountain Way
Grants Pass, OR 97526
(800) 423-2319
E-mail: questions@firemtn.com
Web site: www.firemountaingems.com

Frantz Art Glass and Supply
1222 E. Sunset Hill Road
Shelton, WA 98584
(800) 839-6712
Web site: www.frantzartglass.com

Halcraft USA Inc.
Cliff Wallach
60 S. Macquesten Parkway
Mount Vernon, NY 10550
(212) 376-1580
E-mail: clifford@halcraft.com

Judikins, Inc.
Judi Watanabe
17803 S. Harvard Blvd.
Gardena, CA 90248
(310) 515-1115
E-mail: customerservice@judikins.comwww.judikins.com

Karmul Studios – The Brass Findings Company
Wendy Mullane and Jeanne Holland
704 Park Ave.
Galena, IL 61036
(815) 541-0219
E-mail: Wmullane@karmul.com
Web site: www.karmul.com

Memory Maker Photo Bracelet
Key Item Sales, Inc.
8911 Independence Ave.
Canoga Park, CA 91304
(818) 885-5070
E-mail: info@memorymakerbracelet.com
Web site: www.memorymakerbracelet.com

Polyform Products Company
Iris Weiss
1901 Estes Ave.
Elk Grove Village, IL 60007-5415
(847) 427-0020 ext. 12
E-mail: iweiss@polyformproducts.com
Web site: www.polyformproducts.com

Coiling Gizmo
LeRoy Goertz
P.O. Box 66612
Portland, OR 97290
(503) 775-5242
E-mail: sales@coilinggizmo.com
Web site: www.coilinggizmo.com

Rio Grande
7500 Bluewater Road, NW
Albuquerque, NM 87121
(800) 253-9738
E-mail: info@riogrande.com
Web site: www.riogrande.com

Rubber Stamps of Arkansas
Tracy Callahan
1611 W. Bradley Lane
Russellville, AR 72801
(479) 968-1926
E-mail: tracyc@cox-internet.com
Web site: www.rubberstampsofarkansas.com

Shutterfly
Where your pictures live
3180 Corporate Place
Hayward, CA 94545
Web site: www.shutterfly.com

Susan Jones' Jones Tones
Micro-Cut Glitter
33865 United Avenue
Pueblo, CO 81001
(719) 948-0048
E-mail: sales@jonestones.com
Web site: www.jonestones.com